"... thanks are the highest form of thought, and gratitude is happiness doubled by wonder."

— G. K. Chesterton

The Tumbler of God

In gratitude to Aidan Mackey,
the grandfather of all modern Chestertonians,
who encouraged me to keep writing about Chesterton

ROBERT WILD

The Tumbler of God

Chesterton as Mystic

INTRODUCTION
by
Stratford Caldecott

Angelico Press

First published by Justin Press, Ottowa, ON, 2012
Second, augmented edition, Angelico Press, 2013
© Robert Wild, 2013
Introduction © Stratford Caldecott, 2013

For information, address:
Angelico Press, 4619 Slayden Rd., NE
Tacoma, WA 98422
www.angelicopress.com

978-1-62138-027-6

Cover Design: Cristy Deming
Cover Image: "As I Am," by G.K. Chesterton.
From *The Coloured Lands*, NY: Sheed & Ward, 1938

CONTENTS

Introduction

Stratford Caldecott

Gilbert Keith Chesterton is best known today, at least in England, for the Father Brown detective stories, which were based on the character of a parish priest who received him into the Roman Catholic Church in 1922. Already in 1908, however, as a member of the Church of England, he had written a famous description of his conversion to Christian belief called *Orthodoxy*, which has consistently been voted one of the best books of that century. His other great religious work, *The Everlasting Man* (1925), was a survey of the history of the religious experience of mankind written in reply to H.G. Wells' atheistic *Outline of History*.

As a journalist and later a newspaper editor, an illustrator, a broadcaster, a playwright, a novelist, a controversialist and social activist, Chesterton became a world-famous celebrity, and his debates with his friend, the atheist socialist George Bernard Shaw, would pack the Royal Albert Hall. But he was also a mystic, as Father Wild shows so beautifully in this book, and that makes him, if possible, even more unusual. He had what is these days called a "spirituality," even though he lived in the midst of the world, and (quite often) in the midst of chaos. There is something we can all learn from him.

One of the tests of sanctity is said to be a contagious happiness and inner peace. Chesterton had his share of sorrows and of illness, and his darker moments; but more than most people he was imbued with a kind of unpretentious beatitude that tended to convey itself to those around him. The writer Franz Kafka said of Chesterton, "He is so happy one might almost think he had discovered God." Indeed he had, and he was doing his best to live in the light of that discovery. What was his "secret"? It was to love the splendor of the real, and to live in adulthood the innocence and wonder of the child who sees everything for the first time. The Gospel tells us we must become again like little children in order to enter the kingdom. Chesterton shows us how.[1]

Innocence is a state that has to continually be fought for and which is continually in danger. Chesterton had a happy childhood, but, as a young man, he fell into the fashionable decadence of London at the end of the nineteenth century, dabbled in the occult and became aware of the existence of the Devil. Ultimately he was to find his way into the Catholic Church because he valued the power—the very necessary power—of the sacrament of Confession. It is this sacrament, or rather the absolution it contains, which makes it possible for a grown man to regain the innocence he had when he was only five minutes old.

The spirituality we associate with Chesterton is also a Franciscan spirituality. In his biography of St. Francis the mystic poet, we may catch Chesterton describing an aspect of his own religious experience. But here we come upon a challenge. Is it really possible to compare the life of such a great ascetic, who attained poverty of spirit through the radical renunciation of family and possessions, with the life of a wine-bibbing reporter in Fleet Street, or a married suburbanite in Beaconsfield?

Certainly, Chesterton seemed to *understand* asceticism, at least in theory. For the contemplative vision, he says, reveals the world as it really is by turning it upside-down, and revealing the fragile dependence of all that seemed solid and certain upon the fine thread of the mercy of God, on which it hangs. This is the discovery of an infinite debt, of the kind that lovers delight in: we love to be in each other's debt, and so to be continually paying it back. Thus the saint, who is nothing if he is not a lover, "will always be throwing things away into a bottomless pit of unfathomable

---

1 Hans Urs von Balthasar's insight into childlikeness is very helpful here. David L. Schindler summarizes it as follows: "Finally, childlikeness consists in a sense of existence as play: a sense of the intrinsic worth of each moment of existence. It is this sense of existence as play which reveals the true meaning of time: 'A child knows that God can find him at every moment because every moment opens up for him and shows him the very ground of time: as if it reposed on eternity itself'" (*Heart of the World, Center of the Church*, 1996, 270).

thanks. Men who think they are too modern to understand this are in fact too mean to understand it; we are most of us too mean to practice it. We are not generous enough to be ascetics; one might almost say not genial enough to be ascetics. A man must have magnanimity of surrender, of which he commonly only catches a glimpse in first love, like a glimpse of our lost Eden."[2]

But while Chesterton was on no account too "mean" to understand asceticism, he can hardly have been said in any obvious way to have practiced it. That was not his calling. His were rather the ordinary virtues of a man in the pub who is faithful to his wife and to his friends, generous and loving to all he meets. The mysteries of the inner life and the soul's intention we must leave to God, but, to some extent, we can see the fruits of a person's sanctity in the lives of those around him, whatever his walk of life. God seems to have used Chesterton not only to make others happy, but also to bring them into the Church. He was a convert who gave birth to a multitude of converts.

His mysticism was hidden, perhaps even from himself. But it consisted, I think, in what he calls a "faith in receptiveness" and "respect for things outside oneself." He knew his existence was a gift from God, and his spirituality was one of gratitude, of thanksgiving, and of praise. This is one way, and an important way, in which we may become holy by participating in the life of the Blessed Trinity, which is the life of self-giving love, of continual receiving, and joyful giving. "I would maintain," Chesterton wrote (in *A Short History of England*), "that thanks are the highest form of thought; and that gratitude is happiness doubled by wonder."[3]

In the fourth chapter of *Heretics* we read a clue as to the nature of the "mystical experience" that flows from such a settled disposition to gratitude:

"Blessed is he that expecteth nothing, for he shall be gloriously surprised." The man who expects nothing sees redder

2 G.K. Chesterton, *St. Francis of Assisi* (Mineola, NY: Dover Publications, Inc., 2008), 66.

3 G.K. Chesterton, *A Short History of England* (New York: John Lane Company, 1917), 72.

roses than common men can see, and greener grass, and a more startling sun. Blessed is he that expecteth nothing, for he shall possess the cities and the mountains; blessed is the meek, for he shall inherit the earth. Until we realize that things might not be, we cannot realize that things are. Until we see the background of darkness we cannot admire the light as a single and created thing. As soon as we have seen that darkness, all light is lightening, sudden, blinding, and divine.[4]

There is also, we may surmise, something inherently *sociable* about such a mysticism.

This is not only because we know that "Our God is a society" and that he commands us to love our neighbor (Chesterton adds that while we are told to love our neighbors as ourselves, we are also told to love our enemies, probably because they are generally the same people), but because such a mystic sees people as coming fresh from the hand of God, as dropping out of heaven, as full of divine mysteries, being made in the image of the Invisible and loved into existence. How could we not love them too, when we see them in this way?

For that reason, Chesterton's mysticism reveals itself in his gift for friendship. He seems never to have made an enemy, and even his intellectual opponents found themselves loved, and loved him in return. "All human beings," he wrote in *The Thing*, "without any exception whatever, are specially made, were specially shaped and pointed like shining arrows, for the end of hitting the mark of Beatitude." They are not only coming from God; they are returning to him. The natural creature has a supernatural end. He could see this in them, where most of us do not.

There have been many good books on Chesterton in recent years. His star seems again to be rising, and the number of people writing dissertations on his work is growing. But until now we lacked a book that spoke openly of what is, in the end, the most important thing about him: his friendship with God.

---

4 G. K. Chesterton, *Heretics* (New York: Dodd, Mead & Co., 1925), 65.

Preface

In March, 2010, I received an email from William Oddie. He was preparing a book comprised of the talks given at the June, 2009 Oxford Conference on the "Holiness of Chesterton." He had come across my manuscript, *The Tumbler of God: Chesterton as Mystic*,[1] and asked if he could use a chapter for this book. Needless to say, I was overjoyed and honored. It had been several years since I had done any work on the manuscript, but evidently it was still contemporary enough to be used in a very recent book.[2]

In 1994 I had written a series of articles entitled "Wild about Chesterton" for the Ottawa Chesterton Society's newsletter, *All Things Considered*. These articles were mainly centered on Chesterton's holiness. I was convinced that he was not only a brilliant man but a holy man. I was also calling for a cause for his canonization, and asked for some response to this proposal from the reading public

One of my respondents was in a letter from Aidan Mackey, April 12, 1994:

> Dear Fr. Wild, Firstly, may I say now what I should have written long ago—that I greatly enjoy your *Wild about Chesterton* articles. Please keep writing. The main purpose of this letter is to respond to your request for comments on the opening of a cause of canonization for Chesterton.

He expresses some reservations about such a cause (he may have changed his mind at this present date), but then he said:

---

1 www.fatherbobwild.org. This contains other articles about Chesterton as well as writings about Catherine Doherty and the spiritual life.

2 William Oddie (ed.), *The Holiness of G.K. Chesterton* (Herefordshire: Gracewing, 2010).

On the other hand, I accept that this is one more case of Aidan Mackey imagining that his judgment is better than that of almighty God and his Church! The sensible course, as in all affairs, is to make a tentative move and let God and the Church decide. Being an old man, I am increasingly convinced that the most worthwhile prayer is just 'Thy will be done.' This is not to advocate passivity, of course.

He then shared with me a personal experience. When he and his wife were looking for a house in 1950, "we decided to invoke the help of G.K.C. We did this (making, of course, the normal reservations due to the rulings of the Church) at early Mass." They found a house that very day. In a cause for canonization this would be part of the *fama sanctitatis*—people praying through a Servant of God's intercession because one believes he or she has a special relationship with the Lord.

Aidan also shared with me an earlier exchange about Chesterton's canonization:

> One last thought. I was for ten years Chairman of the Chesterton Society in this country. At one A.G.M. held at Top Meadow in the middle 1980s, Sir James Stephens asked from the floor whether the time had come to have G.K.C. raised to the altars. With the fourth-form wit for which I am renowned (and loathed) I replied "not until the altars have been very considerably strengthened!"

So I was delighted when I heard about the conference, and that some of the best Chestertonians in the world were seriously and more publicly talking about Chesterton's holiness and canonization. It was a great privilege to be asked to contribute to the book publicizing the conference.

The present book is not so much about his holiness, or about his being a theologian.[3] However, after being contacted by Oddie, I was inspired, for two reasons, to take up work once again on the manuscript: 1) maybe my ancient manuscript was

---

3 Aidan Nichols, O.P., *Chesterton as Theologian* (London: Darton-Longman-Todd, 2009).

not yet out of date; and 2) if a good case could be made for his reception of a mystical grace, this would be a contributing factor to his holiness and any future cause. Thus, the topic of this book is very limited but relevant to his holiness: Could a mystical grace have been operative in Chesterton's thinking?

I don't remember when I first started wondering if the quality of his mind went beyond simple good insights, and that there might be some kind of mystical grace involved. Hugh Kenner's *Paradox in Chesterton* has been a significant push in this direction. He showed me the extraordinary nature of Chesterton's mind. At the end of Chapter V, "The World," he wrote:

> Chesterton's analogical perception of Being has led us from elementary wonder to the very heart of a paradoxical universe. It may be said without exaggeration that he ranks almost with St. Thomas himself in the comprehensiveness of that initial perception; and that very certainty and immediacy which makes it unnecessary for him to struggle at any time with any truth and so makes significant dramatic expression impossible for him, places him securely not in the hierarchy of the artists but in one not less distinguished: the long line of exegetists [*sic*] and theologians who have successively explored the same cosmos and the light of the same vision, seeing all things ordered and all things mirroring greater and lesser things: the Fathers, philosophers, and Doctors of the Church.[4]

Ranking Chesterton with the "Fathers and Doctors" of the Church was a quantum leap in my amazement at who Chesterton might be. And when I came across the fact that Von Balthasar, in his Vol. II of *The Glory of the Lord*, "Studies in Theological Style: Clerical Styles," would have considered Chesterton as "worthy of presentation," my appreciation of Chesterton's mind took another quantum leap.[5]

4 Hugh Kenner, *Paradox in Chesterton* (New York: Sheed & Ward, 1947), 102.

5 Hans Urs von Balthasar, *The Glory of the Lord* (San Francisco: Ignatius Press, 1984), 21.

And then I began coming across authors who suggested that there might be more to Chesterton's mind than simply wise intellectual insights. In Quentin Lauer, S.J.'s study, *G.K. Chesterton, Philosopher Without Portfolio*, I read:

There is in faith, not only as Chesterton saw it but also as it happened in him, more than just a hint *of mystic vision,* a seeing of what rational mind all by itself could not fathom. Not only was he constant in his praise of mysticism, whether the poetical mysticism of Francis of Assisi, the theological mysticism of Thomas Aquinas, or what we might call his own 'intellectual mysticism,' but he saw commitment to Jesus Christ in faith as essentially a mystical venture.[6]

Ian Boyd, the editor of *The Chesterton Review* and surely one of the most knowledgeable of Chestertonian scholars, wrote: "What is most needed for an understanding of [Chesterton's] work is *a definition of the special religious quality which permeates it.* (Italics mine) Like George MacDonald, from whom he learnt the Sacramental view of life which altered his entire existence, he evolved a biblical spirituality which is *fundamentally mystical.* Whatever the variety of his topics, his underlying subject is always the same: the presence of God in created being."[7]

This, then, is my limited topic: to try and demonstrate that the special religious quality permeating Chesterton's mind was a *mystical grace,* properly so-called.

I presented this thesis at the meeting of the Southern Chesterton Society in Sussex, England, June 10, 2000. A gentleman, who wishes to remain anonymous, wrote:

Chesterton, true, is a mystic but don't we have to admit this, that's he's rather an inferior one? By this I mean only that real or superior mysticism always seems to be allied to great suffering and while GKC, like all human beings, certainly suffered, one doesn't regard him in the same light as one

6 Quentin Lauer, S.J., *G.K. Chesterton, Philosopher Without Portfolio* (New York: Fordham University Press, 1988), 166.

7 Ian Boyd, "Chesterton and the Bible," *The Chesterton Review* XI, No. 1, 22, 31.

does regard, say, St. John of the Cross or St. Therese of Lisieux. So a saint yes, but despite his wisdom, someone who would never be made a Doctor of the Church, as a deep Christian mysticism cannot leave out a theology linked to whatever meaning we attach to the mystery of the Crucifixion, or can it? (Private correspondence)

I will be trying to answer these and many other objections to calling Chesterton a mystic, but let me give here some brief introductory rebuttals.

Just to mention John of the Cross is to conjure up notions of terrible trials and dark nights of the soul. No doubt many of the great mystics have undergone awful journeys into the caverns of the spirit. However, I do not think this is necessary *in order to receive a particular mystical grace.* The mystical grace I will be arguing for is in the realm of *gratiae datae*, graces given *primarily for others.* They do not necessarily mean that the person is holy. God can give such a grace to anybody he wants to, even if that person has not achieved any exalted degree of charity. Even when we turn to the saints, we find that they are called to various depths of mystical experience, accompanied by various degrees of suffering.

This being the case, couldn't some persons be given a mystical grace without a prolonged dark night such as described by the great mystical writers like John of the Cross? I think so. And could not a person receive a mystical grace without being very holy? I think so. I will have something to say later on in this discussion about the "dark night" Chesterton underwent in the early part of his life.

Many people will not accept a person as a mystic unless he or she is a canonized saint. On the other hand, someone could be a mystic, in several legitimate senses of that word, and not be a saint.

Let me explain.

One rather modern meaning of "a mystic" is someone who experiences extraordinary phenomena, Bernadette at Lourdes, for example. The Church pronounced on the validity of her visions before declaring her a saint. Chesterton thought William Blake really had some truly mystical visions; I doubt if Chesterton thought he was a saint. In a broad rendering of the term, Clement of Alexandria said that every baptized person is a mystic, precisely because he or she shares in the divine life; but we would not consider every Christian a "saint" in the Church's canonical sense of the word.

Some people may even receive mystical graces which may not be part of their normal journey to God. The Lord simply wanted them to have this grace, probably for some mission or purpose. Post-apostolic revelations are often of this nature. The revelations of the Sacred Heart to St. Margaret Mary may or may not have been at a time when she was in the unitive way. The Lord just wanted to reveal his Heart to somebody for this new devotion in the Church, and he chose Sr. Margaret Mary. Such graces can often be validated apart from their sanctity. Chesterton, I will argue, received such a mystical grace and, yes, for a particular *mission* (to be elaborated on). It is the purpose of this book to describe this grace, to argue for it. His mystical grace is not bound up with his being a saint, although I believe he was also that. He once said, "We need a new kind of saint." I say, "We need a new kind of mystic," and this is what Chesterton was.

I hope to show that Chesterton "fits" into at least some of the traditional definitions of mysticism, and that he is as much a mystic as Tauler or Ruysbroeck or Duns Scotus Eriugena. I make special mention of these three men for the sake of comparison, precisely because they are *not canonized*. The Church can approve someone's mystical teaching while leaving open the question of his or her personal sanctity. We have many teachers of mysticism—mystics—in our tradition who have not been canonized.

When we think of "mystical graces," our minds (as did that of my forthright correspondent above) turn to St. John of the Cross or St. Teresa of Avila. These people were Religious in the canonical sense of the word. Nevertheless, because they achieved holiness, many people—laity included—seek to adapt this Carmelite spirituality to their everyday lives in order to achieve holiness.

But for too long lay people have been striving to adapt the mystical spirituality of the cloister or monastery, and have not believed in the authentic paths of *lay mysticism* which are open to them through the guidance of the Holy Spirit. Chesterton has a clear doctrine of a lay mysticism whose time has come. There are many kinds of mysticism, and Chesterton, for one, has been given the grace of an authentic lay mysticism for the Church.

Stratford Caldecott, in his comments about the manuscript, said:

> Speaking for myself, I was captivated and edified in my reading of your manuscript, especially since, like Chesterton, I've never felt particularly attracted to the mysticism of John of the Cross or Teresa of Avila stamp. Your elaboration of Chesterton's lay mysticism, on the other hand, kindled my spiritual imagination and reaffirmed my own predilections and quenched my own thirst for wonder and mystery within a blazingly incarnational Christian framework. Small wonder that my mentor, Tolkien, was particularly indebted, at least, to Chesterton, for his worldview![8]

We have to be careful here. In a real sense there is only one mysticism, that of the Gospel. But just as there are many kinds of saints who lived the Gospel in a variety of ways, so there are many mystically inspired ways to God. Chesterton was an authentic lay mystic. If he is canonized, it will be an invaluable recognition, on the part of the Church, that his particular path of a lay mysticism is also a way of holiness. And—perhaps more importantly—that one does not have to be in some kind of continual spiritual agony to be a mystic!

Chesterton had been in the throes of a very serious illness from which he almost died. He had lain in a state of unconsciousness, and his wife Frances watched at his bedside. One day, when he opened his eyes, she said to him: "Do you know who has been taking care of you?" "Yes," he answered, "God."

We'll never know what transpired during those days of his utter aloneness with God; nor will we ever know many of the deeper communications he had with God. Actually, Chesterton was a very private person when it came to speaking about any of his intimate communications with the Deity. But I believe that for much of his life he was in a profound union with God, with

---

8 Personal correspondence.

the One who, in an "immortally active" manner (his phrase), continuously communicated his existence to him.

The innumerable ways Chesterton articulated his extraordinary awareness of the God who is always "immortally active," has led me to the conclusion that at the heart of his mysticism is not simply the *thereness-of-being* but the *thereness-of-being coming forth.* This is of the essence of his mysticism, and the theme I will be developing.

This mystical insight fits in perfectly with what modern science is discovering. In reading about Intelligent Design for the past year or so, I've come to see that Chesterton intuited what science is discovering about the Ultimate Cause. I will just give two astounding examples of its numerous findings.

Every cell in the body other than sex and blood cells, says Gerald Schroeder, makes two thousand proteins every second from hundreds of amino acids. This process is so complex that, as reported in *Scientific American,* a super-computer, programmed with the rules for protein folding, would take 10 to the 127th power years to generate the final folding form of a protein with just 100 amino acids. *But what takes a supercomputer billions of years, takes seconds for real proteins.*[9]

Every snow crystal is hexagonal but within this basic six-sided shape there are endless intricate permutations and combinations so that virtually every flake is unique. What is the return on investment on such a colossal production? Is there some underlying beauty about reality that has to constantly manifest itself?[10]

"Constantly manifesting itself" is, in the words of this scientist, what Chesterton called "immortally active." He had a mystical grace of experiencing that everything is constantly coming forth from the Creator. I would say that he had a Creator mysticism.

My thesis is that Chesterton had this mystical grace, and that his articulation of reality corresponds to a personal experience in at least some of the technical senses of mysticism. My brief analy-

9 Roy Abraham Varghese, *The Wonder of the World: A Journey from Modern Science to the Mind of God* (Fountain Hills, AZ: Tyr Publishing, 2003), 408.

10 Ibid., 405.

sis, especially of his statements about mysticism, points to the conclusion that his entire consciousness proceeded from more than just philosophical reflection. Chesterton not only had profound ideas that are vital for the future of Christianity, but he also has a mysticism for the common man that is the fruit of a mystical grace.

How can one even attempt to *prove* he had a mystical grace? Well, it certainly cannot be absolutely proven. But John Saward (one of the translators of the works of von Balthasar), said that I certainly can make a judgment about the authenticity of such a grace. He wrote: "Now, while this is not a demonstration in the technical sense, it is a serious argument of the kind that the Church historians and hagiographers frequently have to make."[11] So I contend that a good case can be made for such a grace. That is what this book is about.

Maisie Ward, in *Gilbert Keith Chesterton,* quotes him speaking about his mystical conviction:

> Before the Boer War had introduced me to politics, or worse still to politicians, I had some vague and groping ideas of my own about a general view or vision of existence. It was a long time before I had anything worth calling a religion; what I had was not even sufficiently coherent to be called a philosophy. But it was, in a sense, a view of life; I had it in the beginning; and I am more and more coming back to it in the end: My original and almost *mystical conviction* of the miracle of all existence and the essential excitement of all experience.[12]

This book is an attempt to argue that this "mystical conviction," and what Lauer called "more than just a hint of mystic vision," were at the source of his "new and fiery resolution," pointing, I believe, to a mystical grace in at least some of the technical senses of the word. He said once of Omar Khayyam that "he was one of those who cannot get out of the Presence.

---

11 Personal correspondence.
12 (New York: Sheed & Ward, 1943), 539.

Religion had hold of the man. He could never be alone."[13] I seek to make such a case for Chesterton himself.

Finally, my plan has been to use many quotes from Chesterton. I want to highlight his stellar brilliance rather than my own limping commentary. Also, although Chestertonians may not find too many quotations they haven't seen before, I hope they may find this topic opening some new areas for further study. I am aware that the issues I will be discussing are very complicated; I do not claim any expertise. My hope is that it will stimulate further research by people much more qualified than I. Chesterton's mysticism has not, to my knowledge, received anything like a sustained treatment to date. My second hope is that those who are less familiar with Chesterton may, by becoming acquainted with the depth of his mind and his vision of reality, be drawn to a love and appreciation of him.

Acknowledgements

I wish to thank especially Denis Conlon and Stratford Caldecott. They both meticulously read the entire original manuscript and offered numerous corrections and suggestions. I'm sure this would not have seen the light of day without their assistance. Above all, I'm grateful for their encouragement to seek publication. It kept the flame of my enthusiasm in this topic alive over a number of years.

---

13 Ibid., 235.

PART I

ESTABLISHING CHESTERTON'S MYSTICISM

1

What Was on Chesterton's Mind?

I begin by looking at the quality of Chesterton's mind so that when we come to some of the definitions of mysticism, we can reasonably see how the qualities of his mind, and the expressions of his vision of reality, could be understood as a mystical grace. My argument will be that Chesterton was a true mystic in at least some of the traditional Christian meanings of the word to be examined in the next chapter.

Before I embarked on my own early studies of this question, I had not come across anyone who actually called him a mystic. However, much as Chesterton himself set out like some doughty explorer to discover the already discovered Isle of Wight, my research soon revealed others already calling him such.

Historically, one of the earliest comments about Chesterton possibly being a mystic is in a biography of Robert Hugh Benson, the famous author of *The Lord of the World*:

And Benson read much of Mr. Chesterton, and liked him in a qualified way. 'Have you read,' he asks in this year [1905], 'a book by G. K. Chesterton called *Heretics*? If not, do see what you think of it. It seems to me that the spirit underneath it is splendid. He is not a Catholic, but he has the spirit. He is so joyful and confident and sensible! One gets rather annoyed by his extreme love of paradox; but there is a sort of alertness in his religion and in his whole point of view that is simply exhilarating. I have not been so much moved for a long time. He is a real mystic of an odd kind.'[1]

1 C.C. Martindale, *The Life of Robert Hugh Benson*, II (Bibliographical Center for Research, 2010), 90.

Perhaps the most notable of the early North American opinions about Chesterton as a mystic was that of Marshall McLuhan
in an essay entitled, "G.K. Chesterton: A Practical Mystic,"
which first appeared in 1936 in *The Dalhousie Review*, being subse-
quently reprinted in Conlon's *G.K. Chesterton: A Half-Century of
Views*. I was very much surprised to learn that this was McLuhan's Master's dissertation. He explained that

> when it is seen that there are two principal sides to every-
> thing, a practical and a mystical, both exciting yet fruitful,
> then the meaning and effect of Chesterton can become clear
> even to those who delight to repeat that he stands on his
> head. It is necessary to define the sense in which Chesterton
> is a *mystic* before the relation of this to the practical side can
> be judged.[2]

My book is an attempt to take up the challenge that McLuhan lay
down in that article by sketching out a definition of the sense in
which Chesterton was a mystic. I will be mostly referring to
Hugh Kenner's *Paradox in Chesterton* which is still considered one
of the best books ever written about Chesterton's *mode of thinking*. Thus, I only have a minimal concern with his explanation of
paradox.[3] My main interest is how Kenner describes the *quality of
Chesterton's mind*.[4]

In his introduction to the book, Marshall McLuhan cites
approvingly some of the phrases and ideas that Kenner, a prominent literary critic and theorist, uses to describe Chesterton's
thinking: "a metaphysical intuition of being"; "connaturality with
being"; "his primary awareness of things." In commenting on the
Father Brown stories, Kenner wrote: "As human documents they
are trifling; he took them seriously enough to write them because
they reflect, like everything else he wrote, the unique *metaphysical*

2 Denis Conlon (ed.), *G.K. Chesterton: A Half-Century of Views* (New York:
Oxford University Press, 1987), 1.
3 Cf. Nichols, Ch. 4, where he also gives a brief account of others who have
treated Chesterton's use of paradox.
4 The page numbers in the text of this chapter, unless otherwise noted, are
from Kenner.

intuition (italics added) it has been the purpose of this book to explore." Before presenting the various ways Kenner expressed Chesterton's metaphysical intuition, it will be helpful to know how Kenner explains *what Chesterton saw* with his intuition.[5]

The Idea of Analogy

Kenner says that both analogy and paradox "are tools for dealing with a metaphysical reality that can itself only be intuited. Analogy explores the vision, paradox is a means of expressing it." But both, "unless sustained by vision, unless indeed employed strictly in the service of vision, are worse than useless" (26). I am only interested here in analogy. But what is analogy?

In the simplest terms, it means that two realties share in some quality, only differently: God is good, and so are we. "The answer of St. Thomas and of Chesterton is that goodness is possessed by man and by God, but not in the same way. The way in which men are good is proportionate to the being which men have; the way in which God is good is proportionate to the being which God has" (28).

Kenner quotes the eminent Thomist Gerald Phelan to provide the master key to Chesterton's vision: *"Being is intrinsically analogical"* (27). Kenner quotes a passage from *St. Thomas, the Dumb Ox* that is Chesterton's own explanation of his analogical vision:

> There is no doubt about the being of being, even if it does sometimes look like becoming; that is because what we see is not the fullness of being; or (to continue a sort of colloquial slang) we never see being being as much as it can. Ice is melted into cold water, and cold water is heated into hot water; it cannot be all three at once. But this does not make water unreal or even relative; it only means that its being is limited to being one thing at a time. But the fullness of being is everything that can be; and without it the lesser and approximate forms of being cannot be explained as anything, unless they are explained away as nothing.

---

5 Kenner, xi, xii, xxi, 134.

St. Thomas maintains that the ordinary thing at every
moment is something; but it is not everything that it could
be. There is a fullness of being, in which it could be everything it can be. Thus, while most sages come at last to nothing but naked change, he comes to the ultimate thing that is
unchangeable, because it is all the other things at once.
While they describe a change which is really a change in
nothing, he describes a changelessness which includes the
changes of everything. Things change because they are not
complete; but their reality can only be explained as part of
something that is complete. It is God.

The defect we see, in what is, is simply that it is not all that
is. God is more actual even than Man; more actual even than
Matter; for God with all His powers at every instant is
immortally in action. (31–32)

Kenner says this is "an important contemplative idea; its importance however is the proof it furnishes that Chesterton's metaphysical intuition was intuitive and inclusive. The man who
wrote the above put clearly a point that the merely deductive
metaphysician cannot put at all" (34–35). "His whole habit of
thought began with thankfulness, impelled him to see not lamp-
posts but limited beings participating in All Being; he was accus-
tomed to looking at grass and seeing God. And *the consciousness
of God* introduces another dimension into consideration of grass"
(44). "Consciousness" will figure greatly in the definitions of mysticism in the next chapter of this present book.

In Kenner's last chapter, entitled "The Word and the World,"
he begins with the following statement:

The essential Chesterton is the man with the extraordinarily
comprehensive intuition of being. There is a sense in which
his enormous literary production is a by-product; what must
be praised in Chesterton is not the writing but the seeing. (103)

At the heart of Kenner's thought is the attempt to show that
Chesterton's writings *are not excogitated illustrations of the vision
but ingredients of it"* (103).

Throughout his exposition Kenner emphasizes the source of
Chesterton's thinking: "He never fumbles to reach a position,

because he never needs to reach a position. He occupies a central position all the time" (107). Again: "Chesterton's writing at its best is concerned with fixing exactly a statement of a metaphysical vision, by indicating relationships of word and example within that vision." And later on he reiterates the central preoccupation and argument of his whole book, which is to "explore [Chesterton's] unique metaphysical intuition" (102).

Even before I read Kenner I had concluded that Chesterton had enjoyed some kind of extraordinary intuition of being, and that it was through this intuition that he related to God. In short, I surmised that Chesterton had what I believe is the essence of mysticism: a profound, intuitive awareness of the Presence.[6]

I contend that "mystical" can also be substituted for the way Kenner uses the word "metaphysical." Chesterton himself used the word "mystical" to describe a necessary dimension of seeing the world, but defines it in his own way. My argument is simply that this central clarity that Chesterton enjoyed, whether it be called metaphysical or philosophical or intuitive, can be understood as arising from a truly mystical experience of reality, the fruit of a mystical grace. This conclusion can be valid, even though Chesterton's use of the word "mystical" is not in accord with technical theological language as regards mysticism.[7] He certainly would not have thought of himself as a mystic in any traditional Christian sense of that word; as we shall see, he uses the word to describe a necessary complement to rational thinking.

I am going to use the groundwork of Hugh Kenner's authority and expertise to establish, you might say, the essence of Chesterton's mind. As mentioned above, Kenner concludes that Chesterton had a *metaphysical intuition of being.* He gives it as his opinion that this is not mysticism in the proper sense of the word.

It would never cross my mind to disagree with Hugh Kenner on literary matters, but I think it is well within my limited competence to disagree with him about whether or not this intuition of Chesterton's was the result of reason, of insight, or of a mystical grace. The purpose of this book is to argue for the latter.

6 See Chapter 2 of the present book.
7 See Chapter 4 of the present book.

Being is Intrinsically Analogical

Kenner, of course, speaks mostly about paradox in his book, but, as mentioned, he also treats of analogy, which is my main interest. Analogy has to do with comparison, as paradox has to do with contradiction; for putting things side by side is a necessary preliminary to having them clash. Likeness is at the core of difference. When it comes to reality, we are tempted to think that if only our minds were bigger we could express a clear idea of being. Not so. There is another reason why being cannot be plumbed: "The trouble, the heretical mystic thinks, and the unsuspecting critic thinks, lies in the mind. The trouble, however, lies in reality itself; and is summarized in the statement that being is intrinsically analogical" (26).

Kenner goes on to explicate what he means by analogical:

One may thus put the analogical principle in its simplest form by saying that Chesterton, like the Fathers and the medieval allegorizers, perceived the world as a 'divine animal,' a network of analogies; had, it may be said, an instinct for Being, without which instinct men are not philosophers, conscious of what is, but mere logicians. (35)

Chesterton was consumed by an instinct for being in all its analogical splendor:

Too much cannot be made of the continual rapture with which the contemplation of things inspires him: trees and lamp-posts and hackney cabs and horses and all the other works of God. And the reason that they are wonderful is that they are: they participate in being. (30)

"It is in this way that Chesterton sees paradox rooted in being, and the created world rooted in God." He called this "common human mysticism." In Chesterton this was an intuitive insight, its primary facet articulated as a concern for Being and non-being, the most central of paradoxes:

Until we realize that things might not be, we cannot realize that things are. Until we see the background of darkness, we cannot admire the light as a single and created thing. As soon as we have seen that darkness, all light is lightning, sudden, blinding, and divine. Until we picture nonentity, we underrate the victory of God, and can realize none of the trophies of His ancient war. It is one of the million wild jests of truth, that we know nothing until we know nothing.[8]

Chesterton's primary intuition concerns the wonder begotten of the contrast between something and nothing.

Since I am going to be looking at the various ways in which Chesterton speaks of mysticism, and arguing that he was speaking out of the experience of a grace he had received, the following comments by Kenner are important as bearing on his (Kenner's) own understanding of mysticism.

Kenner says that, in his early writings, Chesterton used the word "mysticism" in an improper way, until he came across the more precise language of Thomism. Kenner explains that

Mysticism properly denotes an altogether supra-rational mode of supernatural experience, and Chesterton never was nor claimed to be a Mystic, in the sense that St. John of the Cross was a mystic, or St. Teresa. His use of the wrong word to express something of which he was acutely conscious, but for which he did not yet know the right word, has given critics cause to align him with the deniers of reason. (61)

My own gloss on this statement yields the following comments and propositions:

1. Mysticism certainly is a supra-rational mode of supernatural experience;

2. True, Chesterton never claimed to be a mystic in the sense of St. John of the Cross or St. Teresa;

3. He did, however, claim to be a mystic according to his own definition;

4. Consequently, in his early writings, he did use the word "mysticism" in a non-traditional sense.

---

8 Kenner, 36, quoting *Tremendous Trifles*.

My contention is that this "acute awareness" of Chesterton's was a spiritual outlook that came to him as the fruit of a mystical grace, different, perhaps, from the graces received by St. John of the Cross and St. Teresa, but a mystical grace nonetheless.

What was he describing when he used the word "mysticism"? Basically, he was trying to define an attitude of mind which preserves the sense of mystery about life and does not try to reconcile or explain rationally the paradoxical nature of reality. He seems, in fact, to have equated mysticism with the sense of mystery (but not mystification). Chesterton's own explanation from *Orthodoxy* (which we will consider further in Part II) confirms Kenner's claim that Chesterton used "mysticism" to describe an outlook on reality that is deeply tempered by this "acceptance of mystery":

> Mysticism keeps men sane. As long as you have mystery you have health; when you destroy mystery you create morbidity. The ordinary man has always been sane, because the ordinary man has always been a mystic. He had permitted the twilight. He has always had one foot on earth and the other in fairyland. He had always left himself free to doubt his gods; but (unlike the agnostic of today) free also to believe in them. He always cared more for truth than for consistency. If he saw two truths that seemed to contradict each other, he would take the two truths and the contradiction along with them. It was exactly this balance of apparent contradictions that has been the whole buoyancy of the healthy man. The whole secret of mysticism is this: that man can understand everything by the help of what he does not understand.[9]

Certainly, this is not what the modern western Catholic tradition would understand by mysticism, which specifies mysticism as the reception of extraordinary, infused graces.

That Chesterton misused the word "mysticism" in his early writings does not invalidate the primary source of his insights, nor prove, somehow, that they were not the fruit of a genuine

9 *Orthodoxy* (Chicago: Thomas More Press, 1985), 46.

mystical grace. Anyone can, in his or her thinking, allow for a realm of mystery beyond rational thought. Chesterton had this, but it was also permeated by a mystical grace. In his own mind he could have misused the word "mysticism" while the source of his vision was truly mystical. He used the word "mysticism" to describe his vision of reality, what Kenner calls an immediate vision about being. Kenner adds that, "his wonder is directed not towards mathematical accidents, like two-headed calves, but at things in their analogical existence" (35).

As Chesterton himself explained, he subscribed to

'an inchoate and half-baked philosophy of my own, which was very nearly the reverse of the remark that where there is nothing there is God. The truth presented itself to me, rather, in the form that where there is anything there is God. I should have been amazed to know how near in some ways was my Anything to the Ens of St. Thomas Aquinas.'[10]

It became natural and indeed habitual for Chesterton to see that all Being is in God; from which it is but a step to the logical and theological proposition that God sustains all Being. He saw, be it repeated, before he started to reason; and recorded not his reasonings but analogues of his visions. (80)

Kenner's strong insistence on the metaphor of "vision" here points to what I would consider a mystical grace rather than a metaphysical conclusion. Indeed, Kenner himself seems to intimate as much in passages such as the above, as well as in the following: "He saw the relevance of God from the beginning and knew where he was going before he got there" (9).

Drawing on the strength of certain passages, Kenner states that

Chesterton has been loosely termed a 'mystic.' It should be plain by now that the analogical perceptions these paradoxes reflect and exploit is altogether different not in degree but in kind from the mode of super-natural experience that constitutes mysticism proper. (85)

10 *Autobiography* (New York: Sheed & Ward, 1936), 150–151.

If I understand Kenner correctly, he claims that Chesterton's perceptions are just as powerful and intense as those of acknowledged mystics—different not in degree, but that they are of a different *kind*. Kenner adduces no proof that this is the case, he simply asserts it. Indeed, it seems equally reasonable and probable to assert the opposite: *that Chesterton's perceptions are the same in kind as those of the mystics*. As I've said above, it's quite impossible to prove what kind of intuitions a person has, or their ultimate source. But one can make a reasonable demonstration of such a position. I believe Chesterton's vision came from a mystical grace.

To sum up: Kenner says that Chesterton had a profound metaphysical intuition of being, of existence itself. He was smitten by this great paradox: *that anything at all should exist.* Kenner maintains that this was not mysticism, inasmuch as we are not dealing here with supra-rational forms of knowledge. I seek to make a case, however, for the position that such an intuition was indeed the product of a mystical grace.

Kenner holds the following two propositions to be true:

1. Chesterton uses the word "mysticism" in his early works to describe the acceptance of mystery in the face of reality.

2. This is not really the technical meaning of "mysticism."

We shall see whether these propositions are in fact true and, if so, examine the ways in which Chesterton does use the word "mysticism."

My thesis will be that when Chesterton speaks of mysticism, he is being autobiographical, that is to say, he is trying to articulate his own experience in the face of the mystery of life. And, to repeat: I wish to argue that his view of life actually flowed from a genuine mystical grace in the technical sense of the word. His mystical view of life constitutes a great gift to the Church, prompting the rest of us to look on the created world around us with new eyes of wonder as a way of relating to God and the world.

2

Squeezing Chesterton
into the Definitions

After this summary introduction to the quality of Chesterton's mind and experience (which will be elaborated upon in the following chapters), it may be helpful at this point to present some of the traditional senses of mysticism. I say "senses" because there is a variety of definitions and probably no one definition with which everyone agrees. I seek to demonstrate that his mysticism conforms to *some* of the traditional definitions. And my approach will be very simple: I will state some of the ways acknowledged scholars in the field articulate the mystical experience; and then, throughout the book, we will see that *Chesterton's articulation of his experience* approximates very closely to these definitions. At the center of my contention will be that his experience flowed from a special mystical grace and was not simply a philosophical conclusion. This opinion is based on the depth and quality of his articulations. It can't be proven, but it can be demonstrated to a probable degree.

Bernard McGinn as
Guide Through the Mystical Realms

As Dante chose Virgil as his guide through the realms of the afterlife, so I have chosen Bernard McGinn as my guide through the intricacies of mystical speculations. In this very brief presentation of some definitions of mysticism, I will be guided by McGinn who is considered by many to be the foremost expert today on Western mysticism. Besides his multi-volume *The Presence of God: A History of Western Christian Mysticism*, he has authored many other books on the topic of mysticism. As well, I will be using him as a guide to authors whom he considers the most reliable and significant, as well as citing some of his own conclusions about mysticism. Most of the authors mentioned will be familiar to anyone who has read ever so slightly in the area of mysticism. I cite them precisely because they are traditional, well-tested, and their works have an enduring value. It is from their authoritative views that Chesterton's mysticism can be seen as very probably authentic. It is not necessary to go into esoteric studies to demonstrate this. References in this chapter, unless otherwise noted, are from McGinn's first volume, *The Foundations of Mysticism*.[1]

McGinn and Consciousness

Note how often *consciousness* will be offered by the experts quoted below as one way of defining mysticism. Consciousness is one of the categories that McGinn also uses to define mysticism. In the introduction he makes some preliminary remarks on his own understanding of mysticism and how he plans to approach the subject. Besides the categories of "the Presence of God" (which is the main title for the whole series) and "experience," he says that *consciousness* can also serve as a method of interpretation. Throughout our discussion, remember that Chesterton would not have thought of himself as mystic in the traditional sense. I do.

> Mystics continue to affirm that their mode of access to God is radically different from that found in ordinary conscious-activities of prayer, sacraments, and other rituals. What differentiates it from other forms of religious consciousness is its presentation as both subjectively and objectively more direct, even at times as immediate. Many of the greatest mystics emphasize the new level of awareness, the special and heightened consciousness involving both loving and knowing that is given in the mystical meeting. (viii–ix)

1 (New York: The Crossroad Publishing Company, 1994).

I seek to demonstrate that Chesterton's articulation of his consciousness coincides with these descriptions of the "heightened consciousness" as characterized by McGinn. I contend that Chesterton had a consciousness of God's presence in created being that was of an extraordinary degree and can reasonably be called mystical according to some traditional definitions.

What specifies Chesterton's mysticism, and gives it its distinctive character, is brought out in another statement by McGinn, where he explains the general way in which mystics gain access to the Presence:

> There is also an objective difference to the extent that this mode of the divine presence is said to be given in a direct or immediate way, without the usual internal and external mediation found in other types of consciousness. (xiv)

McGinn is saying here that the distinguishing mark of the mystic's mode of access to the divine presence is that it is experienced as being immediate, unmediated. In truth, however, there cannot be a completely unmediated experience of God. At the very least, we must undergo any given experience through our faculties, no matter how rarefied such an experience may be. God uses the media of our internal composition. McGinn acknowledges this when he explains in another place that

> human consciousness in its total activity is always mediated both by the subject's previous history and by the mediations necessarily found in all thought and speech. What the mystics are talking about is what lies 'between' these necessary mediations. (xv)

In other words, McGinn is saying that mediation is a peripheral necessity in the experience of the mystic, dross mixed in with the pure gold of gleaming vision.

It is my contention that Chesterton's sacramental mysticism was mediated precisely *in and through created realities*, in and through *external mediations*. The external mediations are a key component of his mysticism: through a special grace his consciousness encompassed the two worlds of heaven and earth, melding them together in an altogether brilliant and original way.

Everyone experiences external created realities, but not many have an enduring and intense experience of the Divine *through them*.

To repeat again the more precise subject of Chesterton's mystical gaze: he did not simply experience the Presence of God in created reality. He experienced, to an extraordinary degree, *the dynamic power of God constantly creating, drawing the created reality into existence, from nothingness into being*. He was intensely aware, almost continually, of the passage from non-being to being, as if every moment was the moment of Creation in the Garden. This is the ultimate metaphysical paradox, in Kenner's sense, which Chesterton experienced as a permanent feature of his consciousness. By an extraordinary infusion of grace, he felt in the marrow of his being that at every moment everything is actually proceeding from the abyss of the creativity of God.

There is an early example of this consciousness of a constant creative activity of God. Garry Wills, in his introduction to *The Man Who Was Thursday*, quotes the following from Chesterton's notebooks in the 1890s:

> The week is a gigantic symbol, the symbol of the creation of the world:
>
> > Monday is the day of Light.
> > Tuesday the day of waters.
> > Wednesday the day of the Earth.
> > Thursday the day of stars.
> > Friday the day of birds.
> > Saturday the day of beasts.
> > Sunday the day of peace: the day for saying that it is good.
> > Perhaps the true religion is this, that the creation is not ended yet.
> > And that what we move towards
> > Is blinding, colossal calm
> > The rest of God.[2]

2 (New York: Sheed and Ward, 1975), p. xv. Note: in his actual text, Wills has "Monday is the day of Lent." In a personal correspondence to me, Denis Conlon said: "Transcription error by Garry Wills: Monday is the day of LIGHT! GKC's handwriting was never easy to decipher."

Chesterton opposed the chaos in himself and the life around him by considering each man's life a re-enactment, day by day, of the first verses of Genesis. Chesterton took as the ground of his hope that very sense of dissolution that threatened his sanity. By the energy of existence things keep re-emerging from dissolution. Creation uses chaos as its working material. Creation is not only *the* beginning, but is *always* beginning. Once one has experienced that nothingness, the emergence of any one thing into form and meaning, [there is] a triumph, the foundation for a 'mystical minimum' of aesthetic thankfulness.[3]

Baron Von Hügel

The extraordinary significance of Chesterton's mysticism, as I hope to show, is that it is a truly *lay mysticism*. So much of traditional mystical theory calls for solitude, abstraction from the senses, and an entrance into the divine darkness. Baron Von Hügel, in his magisterial study *The Mystical Element of Religion*, called this "exclusive mysticism, the world denying variety sprung from Neoplatonic *via negativa*" (295). This is *not* Chesterton.

There is another type of mysticism that Von Hügel calls the "higher inclusive mysticism: It is characterized by a love and appreciation for created reality, the necessity for the soul to transcend all special or ecstatic experiences in the mystical path, a continued occupation with contingent historical reality" (295). This is where I would situate Chesterton's mystical grace. He could look at everything with open eyes and experience the Presence. Everything can be a symbol, an icon, of the Divine. It is a mystical path of this inclusive type that is centered in the realization that at every moment God is saying, "Let there be a tree, let there be a sky, let there be you." "The creation is always beginning." At every given moment things are emerging from God's creativity.

Surely this kind of mysticism is more germane to that which is revealed in the Gospel by Christ, the Model for mystics (see Chapter 6): "*Look* at the birds of the air and the lilies of field." He pointed us to the actual artifacts of his creation and invited us *to*

---

3 Ibid., xv–xvi.

gaze on them and thus be lifted to the contemplation of his Father's goodness and providence.

Evelyn Underhill

Evelyn Underhill's *Mysticism*[4] is the most widely read book on the subject in the English language. (It was published in 1911. Did Chesterton read it?) As a compatriot and contemporary of Chesterton's, her views might be especially relevant to the English character. She understood mysticism as "the expression of the innate tendency of the human spirit towards harmony with transcendental order" (274). I'm going to quote a few passages from Chapter IV of her book, entitled "The Illumination of the Self." It will be obvious how well they describe Chesterton's own expressions of his experience cited throughout this book.

In illumination we come to that state of consciousness which is popularly supposed to be peculiar to the mystic: a form of mental life, a kind of perception, radically different from that of 'normal' men.

Such a consciousness is 'Transcendental Feeling' *in excelsis*: a deep, intuitional knowledge of the 'secret plan.'

To 'see God in nature,' to attain a radiant consciousness of the 'otherness' of natural things, is the simplest and commonest form of illumination.

An overpowering apprehension of the Infinite Life immanent in all living things.

There are three main types of experience which appear again and again in the history of mysticism: 1) a joyous apprehension of the Absolute; 2) the self perceives an added significance and reality in all natural things; 3) the energy of the intuitional or transcendental self may be enormously increased. This consciousness is perhaps the most constant characteristic of Illumination; and makes it, for the mystic soul, a pleasure-state of the intensest kind.[5]

4 (New York: Image Books, Doubleday, 1990). Page numbers in the next paragraph refer to this book.
5 Cf. 232–234, 241.

Rudolf Otto

Rudolf Otto is best known for his book *The Idea of the Holy.* But he also wrote a classic called *Mysticism East and West*, whose deficiencies, writes McGinn, "have not prevented it from having a continuing role even in the most recent discussions of mysticism."[6] Otto posits an introspective mysticism and an extrovertive mysticism. Only the latter concerns us:

> The extrovertive mystic looks upon the world of things in its multiplicity, and in contrast to this leaps to an 'intuition' or 'knowledge,' that is, the recognition of the unity of all things that eventually leads to seeing the vital immanence of the One in everything. (329)

Joseph Marechal, S.J.

He is probably the least known of the authors quoted here, but from what little I learned about his writings from McGinn, my guess is that he would be one of the best guides in explaining Chesterton's mystical consciousness. His definition of mysticism, which is the result of a profound theory of knowledge, seems made to order for this book:

> Mystical experience is the direct, intuitive, unmediated contact in this life between the intelligence and its goal, the Absolute. It is the intuition of God as present, the feeling of the immediate presence of a Transcendent Being. (299)
> The mystical in any given environment consists of a religious experience which is esteemed as superior to the normal: more direct, more intimate or more rare. (300)

Karl Rahner

McGinn says that Karl Rahner "is the most significant Catholic writer on mysticism of recent decades, and has been called the 'Doctor Mysticus' of the twentieth century" (285–86). What I will

---

6 *Foundations of Mysticism*, 328.

quote from him will be especially helpful in any discussion with someone who says that Chesterton was *not* a mystic. Rahner begins his treatment in an edited collection of his writings with this: "There is no generally received theology of mysticism within the body of Christian theology."[7] He mentions that there is "an extraordinary variety of descriptions and systematizations of mystical experience," giving the celebrated Spanish mystics as examples (71). But then he has this comment that I would apply to Chesterton's writings:

> Besides this literature [such as the Spanish mystics], there is another body of spiritual literature, which one may by no means ignore, in which the mystical element thrusts through to expression, time and again, as the ultimate source of this literature's authenticity and vitality, even though here we have only occasional effective testimony to the authors' mystical experience, and, again, no generally received theology of mysticism. (71)

I simply say, therefore, to anyone who says that Chesterton was not a mystic: whose definition is being used? Secondly, we need not think of Chesterton's *opus* as spiritual literature, although, as quoted above, he said he was always writing about God. And, needless to say, there is no great "systematization of mysticism" in Chesterton. What struck me was Rahner's comment that in some literature "the mystical element thrusts through to expression." This is what many experience in Chesterton's writings.

Rahner does, however, offer his own general quasi-definition of the mystical experience:

> In the mystical experience, the 'mystical' subject undergoes an 'immediate' experience, transcending mediation by categorical objects of the everyday, not only of himself or herself but of very 'Mystery' sheer, quintessential Reality, God. (72)

And one of the places where this experience can happen is "in the world": "Perhaps one could conceive of a 'mystical' experience of

---

7 *The Practice of Faith* (New York: Crossroad, 1992), "The Theology of Mysticism," 70–77. References in this section are to this book.

oneness between subject and *world* as such, which the subject might thereupon precipitately identify with a oneness of the mystical subject with God himself" (72). Chesterton's mystical experience flowed from "the world," from his metaphysical intuition that God was the immortally active source of every creature. Rahner treats many other questions that would be relevant to any in-depth study of a person's mystical experiences. For example, are such experiences necessary for the perfection of charity? He would answer no. Are they greater than the gift of faith? No. As a modern "Doctor Mysticus" his opinions offered above are extremely convincing and, I argue, are applicable to Chesterton.

Thomas Merton

McGinn says that "Merton was neither a systematic theologian nor a historian, but he was certainly a major spiritual—indeed mystical—author" (283). I quote Merton from one of the most recent in-depth studies of Merton, *Sophia: The Hidden Christ of Thomas Merton*. It is an understanding of a kind of mysticism that perfectly describes that of Chesterton:

> There is another kind of consciousness that is still available to the modern person which starts not from the thinking and self-aware subject but from Being, ontologically seen to be beyond and prior to the subject-object division. This experience of Being is totally different from an experience of self-consciousness. It has in it none of the split and alienation that occurs when the subject becomes aware of itself as a quasi-object. The consciousness of Being is an immediate experience that goes beyond reflexive awareness. It is not consciousness *of* but *pure consciousness* in which the subject as such 'disappears.'[8]

8 Christopher Pramuk (Collegeville, MN: The Liturgical Press, 2009), 98.

Albert Schweitzer

The great Albert Schweitzer is best known for his *Quest of the Historical Jesus*. He also wrote a significant contribution to the study of mysticism. In *The Mysticism of Paul the Apostle* he wrote: "Mysticism is the individual's 'feeling himself, while still externally amid the earthly and temporal, to belong to the supernatural and eternal.'"[9] And from the text itself, two conceptions that I would *not* apply to Chesterton: "The mystic thinks of his existence under the pure undifferentiated conception of Being, and sinks himself therein."[10] Chesterton, I contend, does not *think* about Being, and does not experience the divine in his own wonderful conceptions of the divine, or lose himself therein. He is closer to what Merton described. Chesterton is not "looking into the mirror of his own mind," thus raising himself above the sensible. He experiences the Presence in the astounding reality of the existence of things which he sees with his eyes and feels with all his other senses.

Schweitzer also mentions the "bondage in the present life to the earthly and temporal."[11] Some of the Greek philosophers thought of the soul as imprisoned in the body. Chesterton did not think of himself as being imprisoned in the body so much as being in a house—a rather large house—that the children had ransacked in a wild party when their parents were absent. He was too much at home in his body to think of it as a prison.

But there *was* something wrong: Why did he not feel completely at ease in the home of his body? Because of the Fall. This doctrine would explain to him the reason for his disorientation. But what was the Fall? Chesterton explains it as a kind of forgetfulness of our true nature and destiny:

The great sin of mankind, the sin typified by the fall of Adam, is the tendency, not towards pride, but towards this weird and horrible humility. This is the great fall, the fall by which the fish forgets the sea, the ox forgets the meadow,

9 *Mysticism of Paul the Apostle* (Baltimore: Johns Hopkins Univ. Press, 1998).
10 Ibid., 272.
11 Ibid., 2.

the clerk forgets the city, every man forgets his environment and, in the fullest and most literal sense, forgets himself. This is the real fall of Adam, and it is a spiritual fall. It is a strange thing that many truly spiritual men, such as General Gordon, have actually spent some hours in speculating upon the precise location of the Garden of Eden. Most probably we are in Eden still. It is only our eyes that have changed.[12]

The Holy Spirit led Chesterton in a quest to regain his sight and overcome "this weird and horrible humility." This was done not by constantly seeking to escape from the body, or to dwell in a world of eternal ideas. His mysticism led him to a proper relationship with his body, by becoming more at home in it, and by trying to put order back into the house of the world. We are more like princes and princesses who, when their parents left for a night out, ruined the house with a wild teen-age party.

David Knowles

McGinn mentions David Knowles, a Benedictine monk and another fellow countryman of Chesterton, as a modern authority on mysticism. In The Nature of Mysticism, Knowles defines theological mysticism as "an incommunicable and inexpressible knowledge and love of God or of religious truth received in the spirit without precedent effort or reasoning."[13] With the phrase "without precedent effort or reasoning" Knowles introduces the question of the origin of the mystical awareness of the Presence, the origin of Chesterton's amazement. I contend the origin was a mystical grace.[14]

---

12 The Defendant (New York: Classic Books, 2000), 13.

13 (New York: Hawthorn Books, 1966), 16.

14 Rahner notes (op. cit.) that it is not within the competence of the dogmatic theologian to explain the *origin* of these experiences: "And then it will presumably fall to the empirical mystic and the experimental psychologist to explain the origination of this mystical variety of the experience of God." The origin of Chesterton's experience must primarily be sought in his own articulation of his experience.

William James

"William James claims that personal religious experience has its root and center in mystical states of consciousness" (291). In his classic, *The Varieties of Religious Experience*, James has documented how frequently quite ordinary people have "capricious revelations of divinity" in things like a sunset, a human experience, or a flower. I appeal to my readers' own experiences: Surely it happens that everyone, on certain occasions at least, has experienced these revelations of Divinity in some area of creation. I believe it is a common occurrence.

It is also our experience that these "sudden revelations" are not moments that we can manufacture in and of ourselves. They come to us unexpectedly, as sheer gifts. We give various explanations to the cause of such visitations; we might even call them mystical moments. But in itself this is not mysticism. Mysticism describes a rather permanent state in which an unusual touch of God breaks into consciousness and remains in a regular or even permanent fashion.

Chesterton's Experience

From the way Chesterton speaks and writes, I believe he was very often the recipient of these revelations. My thesis goes further: He had some *enduring experience*, so much so that he can truly be called a mystic, that is, that he had some definite supernatural grace to always be aware of the Presence that was "immortally active" in created being. I simply contend that the quality of his mind and expressions indicates a source beyond philosophy and metaphysics: the source was a mystical grace. But also, grace protected him: he saw God and did not die—only a mercifully small portion of God so that he would not go mad.

It is well known that Chesterton went through a period of profound mental and spiritual anguish during his early period. Is it possible that it was precisely in this dark period of his early manhood that he received the mystical grace which forever afterwards became the foundation of his whole life and thought? Perhaps it was when he had experienced something of nothingness that it was revealed to him that it is out of nothingness that the Creator creates. It was the realization of the wonder of this passage from nothingness to something which was his "mystical minimum."

A few years after his crisis he would write:

> It is at the beginning that things are good, and not (as the more pallid progressives say) only at the end. The primordial things—existence, energy, fruition—are good so far as they go. We do praise the Lord that there are birch trees growing amongst the rocks and poppies amongst the corn; we do praise the Lord, even if we do not believe in Him. We do admire and applaud the *project* of a world just as if we had been called to council in the primal darkness and seen the first starry plan of the skies. We are, as a matter of fact, far more certain that this life of ours is a magnificent and amazing enterprise than we are that it will succeed.[15]

Perhaps Chesterton knew from personal experience what he would later describe as occurring in St. Francis; and it is one of the best descriptions of his own mystical grace:

> So arises out of this almost nihilistic abyss the noble thing that is called Praise; which no one will ever understand while he identifies it with nature-worship or pantheistic optimism. When we say that a poet praises the whole of creation, we commonly mean only that he praises the whole cosmos. But this sort of poet [the mystic] does really praise creation, in the sense of the act of creation. He praises the passage or transition from nonentity to entity.
>
> The mystic who passes through the moment when there is nothing but God does in some sense behold the beginningless beginnings in which there was really nothing else. He not only appreciates everything but the nothing of which everything was made. In a fashion he endures and answers even the earthquake irony of the Book of Job; in some sense he is there when the foundations of the world are laid, with

---

15 Chesterton, *T.P.'s Weekly* (1910), cited by Wills, xvii.

the morning stars singing together and the sons of God shouting for joy.[16]

Truly this passage soars to the heights of genuine mystical language. Indeed, I contend that it stands as a description of Chesterton's own mysticism. One wonders whether he entered into this "nothing" as a young man and was led thereby to enjoy a constant intuition of the amazing *it-is-thereness of being*; more, the marvelous existence of beings which are immediately passing from "nonentity to entity." He seems, moreover, to be standing at every moment at the "beginningless beginnings" of things. He is aware of things originating, at every moment, from God. For this reason he is always present at the foundations of the world, since every instant bears witness to the act of God's creating power. (Notice Chesterton's reference to the Book of Job. We will consider this in Chapter 11.)

He was amazed at the existence of anything at all, and this was, for him, the "existential proof," if you will, of the Presence; the proof also of the super-earthly. He would have experienced his belonging to the eternal in and through the temporal. Nothing explains why anything at all should be, and that anything at all exists was the truly amazing thing for Chesterton. The "immortally active" God was not only sustaining the creatures Chesterton saw and felt: at every moment God was bringing them forth. This was the essence of Chesterton's mystic illumination.

Plotinus

Plotinus is the great example of someone who taught a mysticism that is intellectually fascinating, but it is a *theory* of reality— "mirrors upon mirrors upon mirrors"—an image Chesterton often used pejoratively, not only in reference to mysticism but also in regards to certain aspects of modern psychology. Plotinus shows profound intellectual subtlety;[17] and, if you live with such thoughts, you certainly can somehow raise yourself above the

---

16 *St. Francis of Assisi* (New York: George H. Doran Co., 1924), 112–113.
17 *Enneads*, trans. Stephen MacKenna (New York: Penguin 1991), 6.5.12

flowing material world. But you don't necessarily need a mystical grace to do this. You just have to be a subtle thinker, and live in this world of positive thinking. Reason alone is capable of such mysticism.

Pure, unadulterated intellectual mysticism is the misguided variety of mysticism which Chesterton meant when he wrote: "When they said that a wooden post was wonderful, they meant that they could make something wonderful out of it by thinking about it. The modern mystic looked for the post, not outside in the garden, but inside, in the mirror of his mind."[18]

One of the most famous phrases from Plotinus is "to be alone with the Alone." The thrust of Chesterton's mystical grace was totally opposite. In one of his earliest poems he was giving a party and inviting the whole world.

I ask you to keep these fundamental descriptions of *one kind of mystical consciousness* in mind as you read the rest of the book. To repeat: I simply wish to offer a reasonable demonstration that the consciousness Chesterton displays in speaking about reality conforms to these definitions. I am aware that there are countless aspects of this demonstration not treated. My book is simply offered as a modest contribution to the establishment of his mysticism.

18 *The Coloured Lands* (New York: Sheed & Ward, 1938), 159–160.

3

Chesterton's Makeshift
Mystical Theory

We have seen that the quality of Chesterton's mind, as described especially by Kenner, can reasonably be held to correspond to the definitions of mysticism presented in the last chapter. It seems opportune, at this point, to present Chesterton's vision of reality in his own words, which I claim flowed from a mystical grace. "Real mystics," he once wrote, "don't hide mysteries, they reveal them. They set a thing up in broad daylight, and when you've seen it, it is still a mystery. But the mystagogues hide a thing in the darkness and secrecy, and when you find it, it's a platitude."[1]

As a real mystic, what did Chesterton reveal? It was his central "mission," you might say, to unveil the realities we see with our eyes. His mystical doctrine concerns seeing reality with open eyes, the eyes of faith. He experienced God mostly in created reality itself. He believed there was something wrong with our eyes which blocked our vision of reality. It was his sublime calling to show us how to see. He often referred to how children see things in an immediate, uncluttered way. As a child we had the simple experience of wonder at the being of things. But we "grow up" and lose it.

If I may interject here a true story. A mom brought home a new baby from the hospital. Her young daughter, age four or five, asked to be alone for a few minutes with the baby. "Why, darling?" asked the mom. "Oh, I just want to be alone for a few

---

1 Quoted by Marshall McLuhan in *G. K. Chesterton: A Half-Century of Views,* ed. Denis Conlon (New York: Oxford University Press, 1987), 1.

minutes." So the mom put the new-born babe on the bed in the bedroom, and the daughter went in and sat down on the bed. The mother kept the door open to keep an eye on the situation. The daughter leaned over to the baby and said, "Now tell me about God. I'm beginning to forget."

Very early, through his encounter with Impressionism (which was for him a kind of dark night of the soul) he says that he formulated, in the throes of this darkness, his own "makeshift mystical theory." I don't know which came first, the theory or the mystical experiences, but here is what he said:

> In truth, the story of what was called my Optimism was rather odd. When I had been for some time in these, the darkest depths of the contemporary pessimism, I had a strong inward impulse to revolt; to dislodge this incubus or throw off this nightmare. But as I was still thinking the thing out by myself, with little help from philosophy and no real help from religion, I invented a rudimentary and makeshift mystical theory of my own. It was substantially this: that even mere existence, reduced to its most primary limits, was extraordinary enough to be exciting. Anything was magnificent as compared with nothing. Even if the very daylight were a dream, it was a day-dream; it was not a nightmare.
>
> What I meant, whether or not I managed to say it, was this: that no man knows how much he is an optimist, even when he calls himself a pessimist, because he has not really measured the depths of his debt to whatever created him and enabled him to call himself anything. At the back of our brains, so to speak, there was a forgotten blaze or burst of astonishment at our own existence. The object of the artistic and spiritual life was to dig for this submerged sunrise of wonder; so that a man sitting in a chair might suddenly understand that he was actually alive, and be happy.[2]

That little girl I told you about was still experiencing the blaze at the back of her brain, but she was beginning to forget. Chesterton's mystical grace perhaps was given with his own encounter

2 *Autobiography* (New York: Sheed & Ward, 1936), 94–95.

with nothingness, when he had completely forgotten the blaze. Then the grace of "being alive" was granted him.

Wonder and the Wooden Post

I find Chesterton's reflections on mysticism in "Wonder and the Wooden Post" especially relevant for my purposes.[3]

One day he accidentally banged his head against a post. This experience helped him to see "a truth about the mysteries and the mystics which I have half known all my life." It was an encounter with reality that led him to reflect upon mysticism and mystics.

First of all, he lists attitudes in his own life which indicate "stars of the seventh heaven, stars of the secret and supreme firmament: a genuine feeling of beauty and wonder; the power of seeing plain things in a kind of sunlight of surprise; the power of jumping at the sight of a bird as if at a winged bullet."[4]

He does not claim that this is a spiritual gift, or that these experiences are due to mystical graces, although I believe they were. His experience of wonder and his power to see plain things "in a kind of sunlight of surprise" were out of the ordinary. They were at the root of his awareness of the Presence; at the root, therefore, of his mysticism.

He then begins a discussion of what we might call mystics who do not see what he sees: "There are men who are religious in a sense too sublime for me. They cannot see the pebble in the pathways, the twig on the hedge. It may truly be said that many prophets and righteous men have desired to see these things and have not seen them." In his opinion, there is a kind of religiousness—"mysticism"—which is oblivious to the beauties of nature. His own gift, he explains, "is a small and special gift, but an innocent one."[5]

People began reading his early poems with the result, Chesterton said, that "I was told that I was a mystic and found myself

3 *The Coloured Lands* (New York: Sheed & Ward, 1938).
4 Ibid., 157.
5 Ibid., 157–158.

44

being introduced to whole rows and rows of mystics." He met "professional quacks and amateur asses," as well as "many men whom history and literature will rightly remember." But "there was something inside me telling me, with what I can only call a stifled scream, that they were quite wrong."[6] What he says was wrong with them is the great key to his own mystical vision:

> Now, what I found finally about our contemporary mystics was this. When they said that a wooden post was wonderful, they meant that they could make something wonderful out of it by thinking about it. The modern mystic looked for the post, not outside in the garden, but inside, in the mirror of his mind.[7]

Here Chesterton is not denying spiritual disciplines such as meditation and contemplation. His difficulty is with the people who are more enamored of the conception of reality *in their minds* than with the reality itself. They don't see the "pebbles on the pathway." He is decrying the failure of these "mystics" to return to the world after giving leeway to their inward focus. Chesterton elaborates further:

> But the mind of the modern mystic, like a dandy's dressing-room, was entirely made of mirrors. Thus glass repeated glass like doors opening inwards forever; till one could hardly see that inmost chamber of unreality where the post made its last appearance.[8]

The reflection of reality in the mind, or the thought about reality, is not the same as the reality itself. There is a danger—not often avoided—that the more a person gazes upon this inner reality, the more the outward reality can dwindle into insignificance, to the point where one is no longer moved by it, for good or ill. One of the perennial criticisms of mysticism is that it cuts one off from outer reality, makes one live in an unreal world—or at least removes one from this outer world. The inner world

6 Ibid., 159.
7 Ibid.
8 Ibid., 160.

becomes so absorbing that the outer world dwindles away into a fine point of abstraction and/or unreality.

Not only that, but this inner world poses a further danger for the modern mind which is not penetrated by faith. The realities of the world actually become something else in the mirrors of the modern mind that is cracked, curved, and distorted.

> And as the mirrors of the modern mystic's mind are most of them curved and many of them cracked, the post in its ultimate reflection looked like all sorts of things; a waterspout, the tree of knowledge, the sea-serpent standing upright, a twisted column of the new natural architecture, and so on.[9]

As for himself, Chesterton asserts:

> But I was never interested in mirrors; that is, I was never primarily interested in my own reflection—or reflections. I am interested in wooden posts, which do startle me like miracles. I am interested in the post that stands waiting outside my door, to hit me over the head, like a giant's club in a fairy tale.[10]

It should be noted that Chesterton is concerned in these passages with the false mystic observing himself. Elsewhere he says that the saints emphasized two things in looking inward: that the self was a window—not a mirror—letting through the face of God; and that they were primarily interested in cleaning the window through repentance.

> All my mental doors open outwards into a world I have not made. My last door of liberty opens upon a world of sun and solid things, of objective adventures. The post in the garden; the thing I could neither create nor expect: strong plain daylight on still upstanding wood: it is the Lord's doing, and it is marvelous in our eyes.[11]

"All my mental doors open outwards." What a refreshingly

9 Ibid.
10 Ibid.
11 Ibid.

strange and unexpected statement to come from an intellectual! For all his brilliance, Chesterton was in dread of having his mental powers disconnected from reality; in dread of not returning to actual reality—the thing that is marvelous in our eyes. Chesterton goes on about the wooden post:

> When the modern mystics said they liked to see a post, they meant they liked to imagine it. They were better poets than I. To me the post is wonderful because it is there; there whether I like it or not. For the amazing thing about the universe is that it exists; not that we can discuss its existence. All real spirituality is a testimony to this world as much as the other; the material universe does exist.[12]

This paragraph also reveals the essence of Chesterton's mysticism. In his view, we cannot explain why anything is; we are aware that we are neither creating it nor keeping it in existence; we do not know where anything comes from; it is simply stupendous that anything at all exists. This is why, as he says, "facts are fantasies":

> Now the mystics around me had not this lively faith that things are fantasies because they are facts. They wanted, as all Magicians, to be the Cosmos. They favoured twilight. But I was never properly impressed with the mystery of twilight, but rather with the riddle of daylight, as huge and staring as the sphinx. I felt it in big bare buildings against walls washed with warm light as with a monstrous brush. One seemed to have come to the back of everything.[13]

Chesterton was amazed at existence itself—the *it-is-thereness* of things, the fact that things simply are. I'm sure that the as yet unrecognized Presence was in his heart when, as a young man of 20, in 1894, he penned the following poem, entitled "In the Evening":

---

12 Ibid. Solovyov said that he didn't believe in material creation.
13 Ibid., 160.

It is the little brown hour of twilight
I pause between two dark houses,
　For there is a song in my heart.
If I could sing at this moment what I wish to sing,
The nations would crown me,
　If I were dumb ever afterwards.
For I am sure it would be the greatest song in the world,
And the song every one has been trying to sing
Just now!
But it will not come out.[14]

Even after Chesterton tears the veil away from the realities
that stare us in the face, they remain mysteries. By showing us
the splendor of existence, he does not explain away its mystery.
On the contrary, actual realities become a most surprising sacrament of the Presence. Even the organs through which we apprehend reality are more astounding than what we apprehend.
What we need is a grace of distance, something sharp and powerful that will cleave us from the miracles that are so close we
cannot see them:

The Sword of Surprise

Sunder me from my bones, O sword of God,
Till they stand stark and strange as do the trees;
That I whose heart goes up with the soaring woods
May marvel as much at these.

Sunder me from my blood that in the dark
I hear that red ancestral river run,
Like branching buried floods that find the sea
But never see the sun.

Give me miraculous eyes to see my eyes,
Those rolling mirrors made alive in me,

14 *The Works of G.K. Chesterton,* The Wordsworth Poetry Library (Hertfordshire: Wordsworth Edition Ltd, 1999), 86.

Terrible crystal more incredible
Than all the things they see.[15]

The Word of God is called a "sword" in the scriptures. Chesterton prays that the Lord, the Word of God, act as a sword and sever him from the blindness which prevents his seeing the splendor of immediate reality. The concluding stanza is a beautiful prayer for a compassionate love of oneself, that is, for the grace to see ourselves as we see our neighbor:

Sunder me from my soul, that I may see
The sins like streaming wounds, the life's brave beat;
Till I shall save myself, as I would save
A stranger in the street.[16]

Rose-Colored Glasses

That our eyes are sundered from the marvels of immediacy is a theme of one of Chesterton's very early writings, *The Coloured Lands*.

Tommy is sitting outside and is bored with the bare, *whitewashed* wall of the cottage; bored with the blank *blue* of the summer sky; bored with the dull *yellow* of the thatched roof; bored with the irritatingly *straight row* of flower pots; bored with the *red* of the flowers; bored with the *greenness* of the grass. Grown-up

---

15 Ibid., 49. "Seeing. A chain of chemical reactions is triggered off when a retinal cell absorbs light. A single photon acting on the rhodopsin protein in a rod cell sets off cascades of enzymatic activities that translate this information into a signal that can be processed by the nervous system. The retina processes ten one-million-point images every second. Through chemical amplifiers it produces up to 100,000 messenger molecules from a single photon. To match the retina's processing power, a robot vision program would have to perform 1,000 million computer instructions per second. It has also been estimated that computer simulation of the processing performed by just one retinal nerve cell in one-hundredth of a second would call for the solutions of 500 simultaneous non-linear differential equations 100 times" (*The Wonder of the World*, 414). This is what Chesterton intuited that the Creator does at every instant!

16 Ibid.

people in this state of mind "go away and write books about their view of the whole world." But Tommy was just ten years old, and couldn't do that.

A strange-looking young man comes along and says he's Tommy's brother (his deeper self?) He says he knows how Tommy feels because he felt like that once himself. He thought if he could make the world all one color, his favorite color, he wouldn't be bored. (The Magicians want to "control the elements.") A Wizard gave him different colored glasses of his choice, but he still wasn't satisfied.

And then the miracle happened. The Wizard was tired of the young man's grumbling and told him to make things the color he liked.

> So I just made a row of little blobs of bright red on the white just above the green; and as I went on working at the details, I slowly discovered what I was doing; which is what very few people ever discover in this world. I found that I had put back, bit by bit, the whole of that picture over there in front of us. I had made that white cottage with the thatch and that summer sky behind it and that green lawn below; and the row of the red flowers just as you see them now. That is how they came to be there. I thought you might be interested to know it. And with that he turned so sharply that Tommy had no time to turn and see him jump over the hedge; for Tommy remained staring at the cottage, with a new look in his eyes.[17]

One of the causes of our boredom is the belief that reality has just randomly been thrown together, without any rhyme or reason; or that it is like a machine that is getting old and rusty. If we believed that each color was the choice of a Great Artist, we would see everything with new eyes of wonder, as if we were looking at pictures in an exhibition.

Chesterton's mystical doctrine is not a romantic, humanistic materialism. There is an Artist behind the colors, just as there is a Director behind the play. Objects are not hard, like bolts, but

17 *The Coloured Lands*, 30.

fluid, like paint. (Physicists tell us that all matter is fields of energy, and not solid at all.) The things we see with our eyes are immediate dabs of the Artist's brush, and events the spontaneous directives from the Director. We are involved in an on-going drama, immersed in a play which is in the process of being acted out. When Tommy realized that the colors he was seeing were the result of an actual choice on somebody's part, he had a new look in his eye.[18]

The poem Chesterton singles out in his *Autobiography* to exemplify the dawning of this luminous realization was one called "The Babe Unborn," which imagined the uncreated creature crying out for existence and promising every virtue if he might only have the experience of life. "The Babe Unborn" occupied the first place in *The Wild Knight*. Here are the last two, poignant verses:

> I think that if they gave me leave
> Within the world to stand,
> I would be good through all the day
> I spent in fairyland.

> They should not hear a word from me
> Of selfishness or scorn
> If only I could find the door,
> If only I were born.[19]

If we can speak of a "born again Gilbert," this rebirth probably happened during his time of darkness, when as a young man he realized—I contend through a mystical grace—that simply being born, his own passage from nothingness to being, was the greatest miracle of all.

18 Ibid., 28–29.
19 *Works*, 243.

4

The Mysticism of Orthodoxy

In *Orthodoxy*[1] Chesterton is not using the word "mystical" in the technical sense of Western mysticism, but to describe an ingredient of what the basic human outlook on reality should contain. He calls it a *"common mysticism,"* his *"makeshift mystical"* approach to the world. Evidently this was the best word he could find to express a necessary dimension of the mind for a sane view of the world. It is significant that he chose this word in his attempt to describe an attitude which reaches beyond the rational, beyond the logical. (Did he have an intuition of a special grace?) Nevertheless, he defines the word in his own way. It is quite striking how often the word "mystical" appears at key places in the book. Indeed, as we have seen, he goes so far as to say that it is mysticism which keeps men sane.

In the first pages of Chapter VI, "The Paradoxes of Christianity," Chesterton says he is going "to continue the current arguments of the last chapter, which was concerned to urge the first of these mystical coincidences, or rather ratifications" (153). Chapter VI describes how Christianity is able to reconcile seemingly opposite tendencies in human existence. (It is often remarked by other writers that the "reconciliation of opposites" is a feature of true mysticism.) Christianity is a welter of *seeming* contradictions:

> But if this mass of mad contradictions [in Christianity] really existed, quakerish and bloodthirsty, too gorgeous and too thread-bare, austere, yet pandering preposterously to the

---

1 (New York: Sheed & Ward, 1936). Page references in this chapter are to this book unless otherwise noted.

lust of the eye, the enemy of women and their foolish refuge, a solemn pessimist and a silly optimist, if this evil existed, then there was in this evil something quite supreme and unique. (164–65)

I point out that he says Christianity "had apparently a *mystical talent* for combining vices which seemed inconsistent with each other" (155). Any stance towards life must be able to reconcile paradoxes and seeming contradictions. This is partly what his kind of mysticism aims at achieving. By returning to his thoughts about suicide and the martyr, about optimism and pessimism, he is led to see how Christianity reconciles other opposites as well.

Another important passage illustrating what he means by mysticism is where he quotes the Lord's teaching, "'He that will lose his life, the same will save it,' is not a piece of mysticism for saints and heroes" (170). He uses the word "mysticism" here to describe a paradoxical saying, hinged on the words "lose" and "save." Also, it is not a truth merely for saints and heroes: "It is a piece of everyday advice for sailors or mountaineers. This paradox is the whole principle of courage; even of quite earthly or quite brutal courage" (170).

I pause here. You can understand this saying of the Lord in the way in which Christian tradition certainly understands it, as meaning that if you try and live in too human and earthly a way, neglecting the higher supernatural principles of the Gospel, you will lose your true life in God. The significant thing here is that Chesterton, through his immediate childlike intuitions of life, had already arrived at another depth of the truth enshrined in this saying: that *risk* is often necessary to preserve one's life even on a merely physical plane:

A man cut off by the sea may save his life if he will risk it on the precipice. He can only get away from death by continually stepping within an inch of it. A soldier surrounded by enemies, if he is to cut his way out, needs to combine a strong desire for living with a strange carelessness about dying. He must not merely cling to life, for then he will be a coward, and will not escape. (171)

This is another example of the principle discussed earlier, that his intuitions from childhood were confirmed in the Gospel. And they apply to many areas of human endeavor, not simply the seeking of the Kingdom.

Because Chesterton was a genuine mystic, he was never satisfied with the rationalist position of resignation to the world:

> This mild rationalist modesty does not cleanse the soul with fire and make it clear like crystal; it does not make a man as a little child, who can sit at the feet of the grass. It does not make him look up and see marvels; for Alice must grow small if she is to be Alice in Wonderland. (172)

All the intellectual positions he had come across to resolve the paradoxes of human existence did not square with his ethics of elf land. The Gospel did. But he had intuited these marvels beforehand.

A mystic must have some concept of the human person:

> We were to hear no more the wail of Ecclesiastes that humanity had no pre-eminence over the brute, or the awful cry of Homer that man was only the saddest of all the beasts of the field. Man was a statue of God walking about the garden. Man had pre-eminence over all the brutes; man was only sad because he was not a beast, but a broken god. (173)

A person enmeshed in the toils of a false mystical tendency tries either to get outside the world—to escape from it—or to become enclosed in the self, in order to protect the self from the world. Hence reality comes to be experienced as a problem, as an obstacle to being at home with ourselves.

> For if there is a wall between you and the world, it makes little difference whether you describe yourself as locked in or as locked out. What we want is not the universality that is outside all normal sentiments; we want the universality that is inside all normal sentiments. It is all the difference between being free from them, as a man is free from a prison, and being free of them as a man is free of a city. (176)

These utterances also arise from Chesterton's mysticism; equally

The Mysticism of Orthodoxy

they are pretty heavy philosophy; and certainly solid spiritual teaching. Some mystics have thought of themselves as imprisoned in their bodies, or in the world. One escape is a "universality that is outside," that is, a view, a stance, towards reality that erects an inner world that abstracts from the outer world. The "universality that is inside all normal sentiments" is what I believe Chesterton achieved, and is another way of describing the mystical grace he received.

If my understanding is correct, this means having the freedom to unleash noble sentiments upon the exterior world. You do not simply have your noble sentiments in your relationship with the *"sustaining principle,"* but rather are able to express them in the world. You have a freedom from within to give vent to them, keeping the seeming contradictions in exquisite balance. "How can a man be approximately free of fine emotions, able to swing them in a clear space without breakage or wrong? This was the achievement of this Christian paradox of the parallel passions, their optimism and pessimism, as pure poetry, could be loosened like cataracts" (176–77).

The final proofs which Chesterton offers for many of his arguments are not what you would find in works of apologetics: quotations from scripture, citations from the Church Councils and Fathers, as well as other approved theologians. Here, as in many instances, he turns to the lives of the saints, the Christian mystics:

St. Francis, in praising all good, could be a more shouting optimist than Walt Whitman. St. Jerome, in denouncing all evil, could paint the world blacker than Schopenhauer. Both passions were free because both were kept in their place. The spirits of indignation and of charity took terrible and attractive forms, ranging from that monkish fierceness that scourged like a dog the first and greatest of the Plantagenets, to the sublime pity of St. Catherine, who, in the official shambles, kissed the bloody head of the criminal; in the soul of St. Louis, the lion lay down with the lamb. Becket wore a hair shirt under his gold and crimson. Becket got the benefit of the hair shirt while the people got the benefit of the crimson and gold. (177–78, 180, 182)

His proofs are from the saints, not from dogmatic theology. You could say these are mystical proofs, because his conclusions are based on the lives of those who experienced the Presence, living the Christian life to a heroic degree. Their lives are more convincing proofs than rational or theological arguments.

Likewise, the final insight of Chapter VI—that orthodoxy is the one angle at which one can stand, while there are many angles at which one falls—is demonstrated from the lives of the saints, and not from abstract arguments. It is this constant appeal to life, to actual experience for his proofs that makes *Orthodoxy* much more a book of Christian spirituality than of dogmatics. Dogma alone would refer to the truths of the faith. But when he said that mysticism keeps men sane, I believe he meant this combination of the creed with an expansive, passionate, adventuresome approach to reality. "Elf land" alone does not say what he means. "Spirituality" or "faith" does not communicate his meaning either. He needed the word "mystical" to convey what he was trying to say. And it is the lives of the saints that exemplify what he means, precisely because many of them were also mystics.

Whose Voice Was It?

The main point of Chapter VII, "The Eternal Revolution," is that we must have some fixed vision of the world if notions like progress, reform, and so on, are to make any sense:

> This is not a world, but rather the material for a world. God has given us not so much the colours of a picture as the colours of a palette. But he has also given us a subject, a model, a fixed vision. We must be clear about what we want to paint. This adds a further principle to our previous list of principles. We have said we must be fond of this world, even in order to change it. We now add that we must be fond of another world (real or imaginary) in order to have something to change it to.
>
> We need not debate about the mere words evolution or progress: personally I prefer to call it reform. For reform implies form. It implies that we are trying to shape the

world in a particular image; to make it something that we see already in our minds. (184)

This fits in perfectly with his definition of a mystic as one who lives in two worlds. He finally received the form in the Church's Creed. What I want to call your attention to now is the nature of his final arguments.

Note that he adopts the style of *a voice speaking*. Such an approach clearly betokens an intuition rather than a rational argument. It comes close to delivering some personal prophetic word he has received in prayer:

> When I had written this down, I felt once again the *presence of something else* in the discussion: as a man hears a church bell above the sound of the street. Something seemed to be saying, 'My ideal at least is fixed; for it was fixed before the foundations of the world. My vision of perfection assuredly cannot be altered; for it is called Eden. I lift my prehistoric legend to defy all your history. Your vision is not merely a fixture: it is a fact.' (203)

I do not say that Chesterton heard an interior locution, as some mystics do. But surely it is significant that, in his final statement, he describes himself as having *"felt once again the presence of something."* Yes, you could say this is merely a poetic device: he makes Christianity or the Church into a Voice speaking the final truth. My point, however, is that his final truth comes from an intuition in the form of a voice. The heart of his proof is not a syllogism or a dogmatic exposition, but a "presence" which speaks to him the affirming word.

This portrayal of truth as a personal voice speaking to us is not mere fancy, nor beyond the scope of normal Christian experience. The Lord said that the Spirit would bring to our minds everything he said to us. We are not alone. The Spirit is intimately involved in our thought processes. That the Lord can speak directly to us is a principle that lies at the heart of our faith. Chesterton's "voice" is a manifestation of the Spirit speaking to him: "You have the Anointing, and you do not need anyone to teach you" (1 John 2:27).

Besides being fixed, the ideal of reform must be composite, which is to say, beautiful. What is Chesterton's final argument for this? Again, a voice comes into play:

> And here again my contemplation was cloven by the ancient voice which said, 'I could have told you all this a long time ago. Only a personal God can possibly be leading you to a city with just streets and architectural proportions, a city in which each of you can contribute exactly the right amount of your own colour to the many coloured coat of Joseph.' (211)

Chesterton understands this voice, now as Christianity, now as the Church: "I said secondly, 'It must be artistically combined, like a picture'; and the Church answered, 'Mine is quite literally a picture, for I know who painted it'" (211–12). The third element which a real Utopia would need is "watchfulness lest we fall from Utopia as we fell from Eden" (212).

> Christianity spoke again and said: 'I have always maintained that men were naturally backsliders. If you were a philosopher you would call it, as I do, the doctrine of original sin. You may call it the cosmic advance as much as you like; I call it what it is—the Fall.' (215)

And the chapter ends also with the voice. Chesterton is speaking about the necessity for vows:

> If I bet, I must be made to pay. If I challenge, I must be made to fight. If I vow to be faithful, I must be cursed when I am unfaithful. For the purpose even of the wildest romance results must be real; results must be irrevocable. (228)

The Voice gives the final argument:

> But again I seem to hear, like a kind of echo, an answer from beyond the world. 'You will have real obligations and there-fore real adventures when you get to my Utopia. But the hardest obligation and the steepest adventure is to get there.' (229)

The Eatable Hero

Chapter VIII, "The Romance of Orthodoxy," highlights the dramatic, story-like nature, of the Christian vision. We are real actors on a real stage, and the final act is not predictable. We have romance and danger and excitement because we believe in hard and definite realities such as a Creator distinct from us, a mind that can know that it knows, a will that can will what it wants, a history that can be shaped for better or for worse—in short, human destinies that are not "damned but damnable":

> But to a Christian existence is a story which may end up in any way. In a thrilling novel (that purely Christian product) the hero is not eaten by cannibals; but it is essential to the existence of the thrill that he might be eaten by cannibals. The hero must (so to speak) be an eatable hero. So Christian morals have always said to the man, not that he would lose his soul, but that he must take care that he didn't. (252)

On several levels, therefore, Chesterton attacks attitudes that deny the Christian verities about God, world, and man, and that turn existence into something about which you really needn't take too seriously. Any doctrine which melts you into the All, or denies there is a world, or says to you, "Why bother, when the end is predestined anyhow"—all such muddled views he is absolutely against. Any thinking which takes the romance and danger and thrill out of life is—to use that ancient and unequivocal word of the Church—*anathema* to him. Some of these areas touch the question of mysticism.

Tibet and Christendom

Chesterton often used Buddhism as a foil to expound more clearly his Christian ideas. For my purposes, some of his remarks in *The Everlasting Man* will be helpful. (148–157) He sees Gautama as a philosopher and not a mystic, and admits that this will not be acceptable to the Buddhists. Mysticism conceives something that transcends human experience, and the doctrine of Buddha does not teach this:

Perhaps a more exact statement would be that Buddha was a man who made a metaphysical discipline, which might even be called a psychological discipline. He proposes a way of escaping from all this recurrent sorrow; and that was simply by getting rid of the delusion that is called desire. (152–153)[2]

He says he used to believe what everyone was saying, that Buddhism and Christianity were the same, until he looked into the arguments and discovered that they were not: "I do not think that there are two institutions in the universe which contradict each other so flatly as Buddhism and Christianity" (242). Recent studies may have found a few more faint similarities than Chesterton knew about. Still, the huge differences between orthodox Buddhists and orthodox Christians have not changed.

Pope John Paul II received some opposition from Buddhists in the form of demonstrations during his visit to Sri Lanka. I found this curious, as I believed the popular prejudice that Buddhists are pacifists. In his book, *Crossing the Threshold of Hope*, Pope John Paul had characterized Buddhism as a "negative soteriology."[3] Apparently the peace-loving Buddhists took offence at that, and demonstrated when his plane landed in Columbo. This shows that the gulf between Christianity and Buddhism is still very much with us.

Buddhist and Christian statues portray the difference: "The Buddhist is looking with a peculiar intentness inwards. The Christian is staring with a frantic intentness outwards. If we follow that clue steadily we shall find some interesting things" (243). "With a frantic intentness outward"—isn't this a description of Chesterton's own mystical gaze?

---

2 *The Everlasting Man* (New York: Dodd, Mead & Co., 1925), 152–153.

3 (New York: Alfred A. Knopf, 1994), p. 85. The whole section of the Pope's book (84–90) is worth reading and very germane to our discussion. It is a papal confirmation of Chesterton's mystical view of reality. Especially relevant is this comment: "Therefore man does not need to attain such an absolute detachment [from the world] in order to find himself in the mystery of his deepest self, since at the beginning of the world we find God the Creator who loves His creation" (89).

The Mysticism of Orthodoxy

Is God within us or outside of us? Both, of course, inasmuch as God penetrates all of reality. It would be heretical to say that God is not immanent in the human soul. The Christian doctrine of transcendence does not mean God is not within. It means that even though he is within he is still transcendent: he is not identifiable with the self. There is not one undifferentiated Big Self. The Psalmist often bemoans God's absence or apparent unconcern because there are areas in the psalmist's soul which, for whatever reason, do not experience the Presence. God is totally, existentially present, but can be experientially absent. He is metaphysically present but not effectively present in every area of the human person, since that person has not yet opened himself or herself totally to his Presence. The person is not effectively engaged with the Presence.

Transcendence, in the Christian view, is not a spatial category, but a dogmatic statement about the Otherness of the One who is totally present. Surely this is the height of mystery to have the totally Other totally present, and yet not experienced. What could be more mysterious or paradoxical!

And when the mystics of all traditions enter deeply into the "interior castle," they do in fact experience the greatness of the human spirit. What even the Buddhists and Hindus witness to, I believe, is the exalted nature of the deep self. Orthodox Buddhism may deny there is a self; Hinduism may see this self as an illusion, but both are reaching for something which we, in the Christian tradition, express as being a *"sharer of the divine nature"* (2 Peter 1:4), and being "a little less than the angels." If we over-emphasize the totally immanent Reality, or identify it too much with the self, we get the kind of mysticism Chesterton detested:

> By insisting on the immanence of God we get introspection, self-isolation, quietism, social indifference—Tibet. By insisting especially on the transcendence of God we get wonder, curiosity, moral and political adventure, righteous indignation—Christendom. Insisting that God is inside man, man is always inside himself. By insisting that God transcends man, man has transcended himself. (250)

Christian mystics, of course, also seek the God within; Augustine, for example:

> Urged to reflect upon myself, I entered under your guidance
> into the inmost depth of my soul. I was able to do so
> because you were my helper. On entering into myself I saw,
> as it were with the eye of the soul, what was beyond the eye
> of the soul, beyond my spirit: your immutable light. It was
> not the ordinary light perceptible to all flesh, nor was it
> merely something of greater magnitude but still essentially
> akin, shining more clearly and diffusing itself everywhere by
> its intensity. No, it was something entirely distinct, some-
> thing altogether different from all these things; and it did not
> rest above my mind as oil on the surface of water, nor was it
> above me as heaven is above the earth. This light was above
> me because it had made me; I was below it because I was
> created by it. He who has come to know the truth knows
> this light.[4]

This is a description of the Christian experience of the Immanent
One who transcends the self; an experience of immanence that
does not identify the self with the Presence.

Furthermore, because God is experienced as Other, the genuine mystic does not remain within, but is impelled to engage in
the drama of existence. The true inward vision opens one's eyes
to the actual world. Augustine was engaged in all the battles of
his day and, had it not been for his illness, might have died a violent death at the hands of the Vandals. True Christian mysticism
is not "sham love": "It is as true of democratic fraternity as of
divine love; sham love ends in compromise and common philosophy; but real love had always ended in bloodshed" (246).

Augustine fought the heretics, the intellectual barbarians seeking to subjugate the Christian mind. This combative spirit flows
from a true experience of the Transcendent God: "The truth is
that the western energy that dethrones tyrants has been directly
due to the western theology that says, 'I am I, thou art thou'"
(248).

---

4 *The Confessions of St. Augustine* (Hyde Park, NY: New City Press, 1997), 40.

The Mysticism of Orthodoxy

Chesterton speaks of the difference between far eastern and Christian mysticism:

> Certainly the most sagacious creeds may suggest that we should pursue God into deeper and deeper rings of the labyrinth of our own ego. But only we of Christendom have said that we should hunt God like an eagle upon the mountains: and we have killed all monsters in the chase. (249)

"For it is Not Well for God to be Alone"

When mystics turn inward, they seek to contemplate God. The kind of God they contemplate is determinative of their mysticism. Here Chesterton is comparing the Allah of Islam with the Christian Trinity:

> The god who is a mere awful unity is not only a king but an Eastern king. The heart of humanity, especially of European humanity, is certainly more satisfied by the strange hints and symbols that gather round the Trinitarian idea, the image of a council at which mercy pleads as well as justice, the conception of a sort of liberty and variety existing even in the inmost chamber of the world. (250–51)

From this conception of the Trinity comes a social instinct. We believe that Ultimate Reality is a communion of Persons; that God himself is a society. And, although it bewilders the intellect, the doctrine of the Trinity quiets the heart. A lonely God can beget some terrifying reactions in the human heart:

> But out of the desert, from the dry places and the dreadful suns, come the cruel children of the lonely God; the real Unitarians who with scimitar in hand have laid waste the world. For it is not well for God to be alone. (252)

Christian mysticism can sometimes become too infected with Eastern thought, with Platonism, or with "vast and shallow philosophies, the huge syntheses of humbug, all talk about ages and evolution and ultimate development. The eons are easy enough to think about, anyone can think about them" (252). False mystics can then lose the danger and precarious nature of human destinies and settle into false hope for themselves and others:

> To hope for all souls is imperative; and it is quite tenable that their salvation is inevitable. It is tenable, but it is not specially favourable to activity or progress. Our fighting and creative society ought rather to insist on the danger of everybody, on the fact that every man is hanging by a thread or clinging to a precipice. To say that all will be well anyhow is a comprehensible remark: but it cannot be called the blast of a trumpet. (252)

The phrase *"all will be well,"* of course, comes from Chesterton's compatriot, Julian of Norwich. He probably was not too keen to use her as an example of Christian mysticism because he might have found her too passive, or too socially indifferent to the drama of life. There is always danger of ultimate ruin. Being absorbed with the "God within" can anesthetize the soul to the peril of other souls; indeed, the peril the soul herself may be in. I am not claiming that this is the mysticism of Julian; I don't know enough about her. But indifference to the needs of others, a failure to be involved in the drama of the world, is a perennial criticism of mysticism.

However, in defense of Julian's outlook, we should note that Chesterton did say that the "triple enigma [of the Trinity] is as comforting as wine and open as an English fireside" (251). And, in *The Everlasting Man,* he says of St. Athanasius:

> He was fighting for that very balance of beautiful interdependence and intimacy, in the very Trinity of the Divine Nature, that draws our hearts to the Trinity of the Holy Family. His dogma, if the phrase be not misunderstood, turns even God into a Holy Family. [This] idea of balance in the deity, as of balance in the family, makes the creed a sort of sanity, and that sanity the soul of civilization.[5]

Some mystics are called to witness to our relationship to the Divine Mystery within. One day we will be forever feasting at the

---

5 *The Everlasting Man* (New York: Dodd, Mead & Co., 1925), 227–228.

hearth of the Holy Family of the Trinity. The gentle maid of Norwich witnesses to this peaceful dimension of our relationship to God which flows from sitting in the presence of Divine Sanity and Peace.

It is a further mark of the mystical "reconciliation of opposites" in the Church that the maid of Norwich and the maid of Orleans can both be inspired by the same mysticism of the Gospel. Chesterton probably thought that Dame Julian just sat too long in the comfort of the Fire's Presence like Mary, Lazarus's sister. (Even when Jesus came on the occasion of her brother's death, "Mary stayed in the house.")

> If we want, like the Eastern saints, merely to contemplate how right things are, of course we shall only say that they must go right. But if we particularly want to make them go right, we must insist that they may go wrong. (255)

He preferred the maid of Orleans attacking the battlements to the maid of Norwich contemplating the final victory feast. I'm sure Chesterton was not against the gentle recluses who, like Julian, were scattered around Norwich. But he would most certainly be concerned if they prayed only for themselves and not also for the world.

Having written fragments of a play on St. Anthony of the Desert, Chesterton would not either be against the hermit in the cave. But he would undoubtedly be concerned if the hermit, after his enlightenment, started teaching that social relations with others are impossible, or that sexuality is inhuman, or that everyone should live in a cave. Chesterton is always concerned with the inner attitudes of the mystics, and the principles they deduce from their experiences. He is watchful lest their gazing produce attitudes and theories which are contrary to the basic instincts of all humanity. He would have appreciated St. Paul the Hermit, the first to dwell in the Egyptian desert; but he was more attracted to mystics like Joan of Arc, Francis of Assisi, Thomas Aquinas, and Catherine of Siena, who were engaged in the great battles of their day. His preference was for the battling mystics, those who "sounded trumpets."

Mere Spirituality

I still remember how taken aback I was when I read, in Chesterton's book *St. Thomas Aquinas,* that the Poverello and St. Thomas had saved us from a dreadful doom, namely, *spirituality.*[6] "Franciscan Spirituality," "Carmelite Spirituality," "Jesuit Spirituality"—these were labels I had heard all my life. What was wrong with *spirituality*? Aren't we trying to be spiritual, lead a spiritual life? What does he mean, "save us from spirituality"?

Well, even before the appearance of *St. Thomas Aquinas,* Chesterton, after stating his belief in spiritual phenomena such as miracles, had written the equally shocking words in *Orthodoxy:*

> Given this conviction that the spiritual phenomena do occur (my evidence for which is complex but rational), we then collide with one of the worst mental evils of the age. The greatest disaster of the nineteenth century was this: that men began to use the word 'spiritual' the same as the word 'good.' They thought that to grow in refinement and uncorporeality was to grow in virtue. When scientific evolution was announced, some feared that it would encourage mere animality. It did worse: it encouraged mere spirituality. (284)

As I made my way through his comments on mysticism, I began to see that the above quote was one of the keys to his thought. It's quite a claim that the greatest disaster of the nineteenth century was the encouragement of *mere spirituality.* In the early centuries of Christianity, Platonism and Neo-Platonism had a "spiritualizing effect," and the debates still rage whether this was good or bad for Christianity.

Karl Rahner said that the increasingly rarefied understanding of prayer in the early centuries was due to the Greek theory of knowledge: the more knowledge abstracted from the physical world, the purer it was. Thus, "more perfect" came to mean "more abstract." The more one's prayer was free of sensory images, the purer it was. Accordingly, to have no images or ideas at all would amount to the highest form of prayer. But this kind

6 (New York: Image, Doubleday, 1956), 28.

of prayer was a far cry from the earthiness of the psalmist, who exclaims: "I lift my eyes to the mountains, whence shall come my help?" or the practical earthiness of the prayer of prayers: "Father, give us this day our daily bread."

Chesterton asserts that, in the nineteenth century, this spiritualizing was a direct result of the theory of evolution. Men thought that they were evolving more and more from the animal to the angelic. "But," Chesterton explains with his customary aplomb, "you can pass from the ape and go to the devil" (284). This is a syndrome that can occur in prayer and mysticism as well. You can pass from a sound divine-human encounter to "mere spirituality."

What he is saying, in effect, is that you can encounter all kinds of spirits in the spirit world, but you have to discern the good from the bad:

There are, one must suppose, spirits of all shapes and sizes. So, if we see spiritual facts for the first time, we may mistake who is uppermost. We must have a long historic experience in supernatural phenomena—in order to discover which are really natural. (285)

In *The Catholic Church and Conversion* he says spiritualism was seen as "the only way into the promised land, a future life. We did not like dark rooms and dubious mediums and ladies tied up with rope, but we were told there was no other way to reach a better world."[7] These excursions into the spiritual world led people to a false spirituality, a *mere spirituality*, making people despise the good things of the world. The spiritual became an unqualified replacement of the good.

Chesterton found the true spirituality under the guidance of the Church, which believed "in living in the world with two orders, the supernatural and the natural" (88). We always come back to the same vision, which calls for us to live in two worlds: "The dilemma is how to live in the seen and unseen worlds without despising or overemphasizing either" (88).

7 *The Catholic Church and Conversion* (New York: The Macmillan Company, 1929), 103.

In his treatment of St. Francis, Chesterton would come to use the image of tumbling to speak of his mysticism: Francis made a complete somersault and landed on his feet a new man. That image is introduced at the very end of *Orthodoxy*, sixteen years earlier:

> All the real arguments about religion turn on the question of whether a man who was born upside down can tell when he comes right way up. The primary paradox of Christianity is that the ordinary condition of man is not his sane or sensible condition; that the normal itself is an abnormality. That is the inmost philosophy of the Fall. (294)

Orthodoxy is Chesterton's account of how he tumbled around in the confusion of the world and was able to land on his feet through his discovery of Christianity, which had, of course, already been discovered. In the following passage he uses the word "sceptic," but we could construe it to stand for "modern man," or "everyman," really. We are born with our feet somewhat on the ground because of our childlikeness. Sooner or later, however, all of us are turned on our head by the destabilizing effects of the Fall. It is only the mysticism of Christianity which enables us to stand upright again as children of God—more, as kings and queens:

> The sceptic may truly be said to be topsy-turvy; for his feet are dancing upwards in idle ecstasies, while his brain is in the abyss. To the modern man the heavens are actually below the earth. The explanation is simple; he is standing on his head; which is a very weak pedestal to stand on. But when he has found his feet again he knows it. Christianity satisfies suddenly and perfectly man's ancestral instinct for being right way up. (297)

PART II

TRUE MYSTICS, OR LANDING ON ONE'S FEET

5

The Everlasting Man: Model for Mystics

When I turned to Chesterton's *The Everlasting Man*,[1] his book about Christ, to see what I could discover about mysticism, I did not find very much about "traditional mysticism." Instead, what I found was a *Mystical Person*, a portrait of a human nature perfectly penetrated with the Presence, living very "naturally" in two worlds. In short, I found the Model Mystic.

We have developed, over centuries of Christian reflection and experience, a certain technical conception of what mysticism is. Now, armed with these studies, we go back to the Gospels to see if Jesus was a mystic! Of course, it should be the other way round: the Lord's Person, life and teaching should be seen as defining true mysticism—what it means to be immediately penetrated with the Presence—since he was the Presence Incarnate. He is the True Mystic, and our theories about mysticism should be based on his life, teachings, and approach to reality.

For anyone who believes that Christ was the Second Person of the Blessed Trinity, there is no need to "prove" he was a mystic. If mysticism means anything it means the immediate experience of the Presence. Jesus, of course, is beyond this definition: Jesus *is* the Presence, and is in an unimaginable immediate union with the Father. In many of his sayings he testifies to his immediate presence to the Father: "No one knows the Son except the Father, just as no one know the Father except the Son" (Matt. 11:27); "Anyone who has seen me has seen the Father" (John 14:9);

---

1 (New York: Dodd, Mead & Co., 1925). Page references are to this book unless otherwise noted.

"I am in the Father and the Father is in me" (John 14:10); "I came
from the Father and entered the world" (John 16:28); "Father, just
as you are in me and I am in you" (John 17:21); "I and the Father
are one" (John 10:30). And if Christ is the Mystic *par excellence*, of
course there is mysticism in his teaching, and all further mysticism must be judged by the articulation of his experience of his
relationship with the Father and the Holy Spirit. There is no need
to go into his teachings about union with God. One only needs
to meditate on his discourse at the Last Supper. I am mostly
interested here in Chesterton's view of Christ the Mystic.

Chesterton would have been delighted with the ironies of this
debate. He often expressed, throughout his writings—as we are
seeing—many reservations about traditional mystics and mysticism. There was altogether too much mystification swirling
around them. That is why he would have certainly come down
on the side of the argument which says: "Of course there is mysticism in Christ's life and teaching. But let us look at the Gospel
with new eyes and see what mysticism really is, not what the the-
orists have decided it should be."[2]

Christ worked miracles. For some people this is a sign of a mystic. In our theology of mysticism, however, miracles are not necessarily a sign that the person is a mystic. But there is a difference
even here: when Christ performs miracles he does so effortlessly,
one could say almost naturally, without any spiritual fire-works.
And when he prays, he is not transfixed in ecstasies or elevated off
the ground like many mystics. He prays quite naturally, speaking
intimately to God as his Father; and probably with his eyes open.

In *The Everlasting Man*, Chesterton makes this pithy observation: "Relatively speaking, it is the Gospel that has the mysticism

2 The reader may be thinking of the Transfiguration as an objection to the
"non-mystical" character of Christ. Several observations. Christ is not in
ecstasy *away* from the apostles. They are *sharing* in his experience since they
see him speaking with Moses and Elias. And precisely he is *speaking* with
them, carrying on a normal conversation about his *transitus*, his passing over.
The apostles are not watching someone in a detached "mystical" experience,
but they are with him in this other realm, so much so that they want to remain
in it. The characteristics surrounding the Transfiguration are simply different
from the ecstasies of the saints.

and the Church that has the rationalism" (189), meaning (in my words), "Christ is the true Mystic. It is some of the theologians and philosophers with their rational and intricate systems which have often distanced people from a real immediate contact with the Presence."

The whole approach of *The Everlasting Man* is an attempt to see Christ as if for the first time, with the eyes of a modern person who has no previous knowledge of Christ. If we also look with these new eyes at the "mysticism" of Christ, we may find a number of things which do not fit many of our preconceived and traditional notions. This is because the eyes of many modern persons are clouded over by a dense fog of rationalism and "mystification" about the interior life.

Let us posit a statement with which no orthodox Christian would disagree: "Christ was the perfect embodiment of union with the Presence, since he was the second Person of the Trinity." As he says, "I and the Father are one." However one wishes to express our normal human tension in the attempt to live in this Presence—tension between the active and contemplative life, the natural and the supernatural, time and eternity, the absolute world of ideas and the temporary flux—Christ was the perfect living harmony of these experienced dichotomies, since he was God in the flesh. One would suppose, therefore, that it ought to be *his life and actions* that set the standard for mysticism rather than some abstruse theory into which he does not fit. The life of Christ, who was true God and true Man, provides us with the perfect picture of *the* true mystic.

In his attempt to see Christ through the eyes of a modern reader, Chesterton suspends his own faith. The intent of his presentation is that if you have a preconceived notion that Christ is *only human*, the Gospels themselves, at face value, belie that estimation.

What Chesterton says about Christ in *The Everlasting Man* provides a striking contrast with popular views of mystics and mysticism. It is useful, at this stage of our inquiry, to review some of the passages in *The Everlasting Man*, not in order to arrive at a mystical doctrine, but to show what a true mystic is and draw some trenchant comparisons.

During his life we find that Jesus grew in his humanity. (We leave aside the much disputed question whether or not his *divinity* was affected.) He was always in immediate contact with the Presence—with his Father and with the Holy Spirit. The question that arises is: What did such a perfect mystic in our world look like? Chesterton begins with "unmiraculous and even unnoticed and inconspicuous parts of the story" (188), which is to say, the hidden life of Nazareth.

When Chesterton spoke about mystics like St. Francis and St. Anthony of the Desert, he mentioned how they went into caves and had their initiations into the mystical life. The Buddha, also, in order to be enlightened, left his family in search of ultimate wisdom, finally receiving it under the Bodhi tree. Humanly speaking, and according to the traditional scenario, we would expect Jesus to go through some such period of discipline and purification, like all the other great religious founders.

This is *not* what happened:

> There is that long stretch of silence in the life of Christ up to the age of thirty. It is of all silences the most immense and imaginatively impressive. But it is not the sort of thing that anybody is particularly likely to invent in order to prove something. The ordinary trend of hero-worship and myth-making is much more likely to say the precise opposite. (186)

A myth-maker would be more likely to say that Jesus, after about twenty years or so in Nazareth, went into the Judean wilderness for ten years, and that there, through extreme fasting and detachment from all worldly things, he achieved an enlightenment for his public mission. (Incidentally, John the Baptist is often considered to fit the requirements of this traditional ascetical way. And some would make Jesus a member of the Qumran ascetic community in the Judean desert. But our whole tradition is against it.) After this long monastic discipline, according to this familiar path of the great religious founders, he would have gone forth to teach what he had learned in his wilderness cave, once he had been purified and enlightened.

This is not at all what happened. We don't see the Lord going through a rigorous monastic formation with the Essenes; nor does he spend ten years wandering the world in search of wisdom, like the Buddha. The tradition is that he lived such an ordinary, human existence at home that, when he did start to preach, his own townspeople wondered "where he got it all." Even they couldn't believe he got it all in their own home town. They, better than anyone else, knew the straitened levels of religious and cultural attainment in Nazareth.

Christ did not have to go through all the mystical tumblings of other mystics. He did not have to rise into the center of the divine cloud and descend again, nor did he have to burrow so deeply into the human condition as to come out on the other side. From the moment of his conception, he was in union with the Father. At the age of twelve he says things like, "Did you not know I must be about my Father's business?" which completely baffled his holy parents. His comment indicates that he was living in some other realm; or rather, he was "naturally" living perfectly in both realms, which is precisely Chesterton's definition of a mystic.

It has often been remarked, in a variety of ways, that the final stage of true mysticism is a great simplicity:

> But one thing is clear; namely, that the higher stages of the mystical life are very ordinary. There is no ecstasy, no rapture, no flash of light, no bells, no incense. It is a very quiet and simple realization that God is my Father and I, another Christ, am truly his son or his daughter, and that the Holy Spirit dwells in me.[3]

If you met a person at this stage you might not know that you were meeting a mystic. And the person surely would not know, or even care, if he was a mystic or not. After all the spiritual tumblings and experiences, the true mystic comes round again with simply being a *person*, although now everything is wonderfully different. Jesus in Nazareth at least fits the above definition of a mystic: utter simplicity of life. He started out that way; it was not the termination of a long journey.

3 William Johnston, *The Inner Eye of Love: Mysticism and Religion* (San Francisco: Harper and Row, 1978), 37–38.

Chesterton cites some examples of the Lord's teachings—the Unjust Steward, "not peace but a sword," virginity, the indissolubility of marriage—and characterizes these sayings thus:

> I am dwelling on the dark or dazzling or defiant or mysterious side of the Gospel words. In short, we can say that these ideals are impossible in themselves. Exactly what we cannot say is that they are impossible for us. They are rather notably marked by a mysticism which, if it be a sort of madness, would always have struck the same sort of people as mad. (192)

It should be noted that he uses the word "mysticism" not about a teaching of Christ which proceeds from an experiential contact with the All, or about a method of how to become absorbed into union with God. Instead, Chesterton uses the word in reference to a teaching that points to another world, while being enmeshed very much in this one. The Lord said, "What God has joined together no man must separate":

> Christ in his view of marriage does not in the least suggest the condition of Palestine in the first century. It was much more puzzling to people then than to people now. Jews and Romans and Greeks did not believe, and did not even understand enough to disbelieve, the mystical idea that the man and the woman had become one sacramental substance. (193)

Once again, it is instructive to see how Chesterton uses the word "mystical." It certainly refers to things unseen, but also to realities very much enfleshed: a man and a woman forming one sacramental substance. Christ spoke about things in a way quite different from his own culture and times:

> He never used a phrase that made his philosophy depend even upon the very existence of the social order in which he lived. He spoke as one conscious that everything was ephemeral, including the things that Aristotle thought eternal. By that time the Roman Empire had come to be merely the *orbis terrarum*, another name for the world. But he never made his morality dependent on the existence of the Roman

Empire or even on the existence of the world. 'Heaven and earth shall pass away, but my words shall not pass away.' (194)
   [The sacrament of marriage] is an ideal altogether outside time; difficult at any period; impossible at no period. In other words, if anyone says it is what might be expected of a man walking about in that place at that period, we can quite fairly answer that it is much more like what might be the mysterious utterance of a being beyond man, if he walked alive among men. (195)

The truth about Christ that emerges from Chesterton's presentation is that Christ lived effortlessly in the two worlds of the earthly and the heavenly. With deft ease, Christ creates masterpieces of literature by going, for example, in a consummate, threefold movement from the lilies of the field to a crowning utterance: "And if God so clothes the grass that today is and tomorrow is cast into the oven—how much more you." By means of this stunning progression of images, Chesterton points out, man is "lifted by three infinities above all other things" (200). Christ's "far-flung comparisons suggest something very vast, subtle and superior, something that is capable of long views and even double meanings" (200). No one, be it Moses or Mahomet or Buddha, ever said, "before Abraham was, I am"; and yet he says it "calmly and almost carelessly, like one looking over his shoulder" (197).
   He casts out demons, again, effortlessly: "Come out of him." He is not wrestling with the demons as Jacob wrestled with the angel. There is no combat taking place, but deliberate, calm authority. "The Jesus of the New Testament seems to me to have in a great many ways the note of something superhuman; that is, of something human and more than human" (203). And contrasting him again with the Buddha, Chesterton highlights the essential difference between the two mysticisms:

Buddha did arrest attention by one gesture; it was the gesture of renunciation, and therefore in a sense of denial. But by one dramatic negation he passed into a world of negation that was not dramatic; which he would have been the first to insist was not dramatic. Here again we miss the particular moral importance of the great mystic if we do not see the distinction; that it was his whole point that he had done with drama, which consists of desire and struggle and generally of defeat and disappointment. He passes into peace and lives to instruct others how to pass into it. (205–06)

This is emphatically *not* the mysticism of Christ. Jesus does not teach us, nor does his life exemplify, how to escape into a life of peace and aloofness from the world. ("Do not suppose that I have come to bring peace on the earth. Not peace, I tell you, but a sword.") Rather, Chesterton notes:

Now, compared [to the Buddha] the life of Jesus went as swift and straight as a thunderbolt. It was above all things dramatic; it did above all things consist in doing something that had to be done. The goal that he was seeking was death. The story of Christ is the story of a journey, almost in the manner of a military march; certainly in the manner of a quest of a hero moving to his achievement or his doom. (206–07)

In prayer, the Lord was surely totally absorbed in intimacy with his Father. But this absorption is not like that of many of the mystics, totally insensitive to what is going on around them; or even lifted above the ground in levitation. The Gospel often tells us he prayed while in the company of his disciples. It's a very probable theory that unusual manifestations such as ecstasy and levitation are due to the *weakness* of human nature, unable to sustain the Presence. Christ manifests the perfection of our nature, at home with the Presence.[4]

---

4 Rahner, op. cit., in a section entitled "Everyday Mysticism," says: "It seems to me to be the task of the Christian theology of mysticism to show and render intelligible the fact that the real basic phenomenon of mystical experience of transcendence is present as innermost sustaining ground (even though unnoticed) in the simple act itself of Christian living in faith, hope, and love" (70). If I understand him correctly, he is saying that through the theological virtues, we have within us the essence of mysticism, whether or not it is manifested in special outward graces. Christ, in his union with the Father, was essentially a Mystic, unknown as he was in Nazareth.

I've often remarked that one of the criticisms of mystics is their neglect of the world. Christ's life and prayer did not make him neglect "being about his Father's business" on earth.

Chesterton, in the quote above, characterized Christ's life as a *"military march."* Christ said the gates of hell would not prevail against his Church. It is the gates of hell that are under attack. Christ's military march is an offensive maneuver, an attacking movement, being opposed by a force active in its resistance.

His public life constituted the greatest armada in history, setting out to do battle with all the forces of evil arrayed against him. Buddha, on the other hand, was passive before evil (which perhaps he considered did not really exist). Christ actively confronts Satan and all his minions, who are very real. Christ has come to do battle with them. Christ's is a mysticism of combat against evil in the name of God.

In the chapter of *The Everlasting Man* entitled "The Witness of the Heretics," Chesterton shows how modern criticisms of early Christianity really apply most aptly to the very heresies which the Church defeated. It was precisely the Church which stood fast against the grotesque distortions of the heresiarchs, defying the spirit of the age. The Church had the key. If Platonists or anybody else thought of the human person as being in a prison, the Church had "the key that could unlock the prison of the whole world; and let in the white light of liberty" (213).

As we have seen (Chapter 4), Chesterton often brings up the matter of asceticism when speaking of mystics, since the two are closely related: asceticism is one of the primary ways through which people seek to foster an experience of the Presence. Asceticism is one of the examples Chesterton uses to illustrate his point about the Church as Keeper of the Keys. His comments clarify his understanding of the difference between false and true asceticism.

Chesterton rehearses some of the objections urged against the Church and then points out that the Church was not the guilty party:

Nothing is more common, for instance, than to find such a modern critic writing something like this: 'Christianity was above all a movement of ascetics, a rush into the desert, a refuge in the cloister, a renunciation of all life and happiness; and this was a part of a gloomy and inhuman reaction against nature itself, a hatred of the body, a horror of the material universe, a sort of universal suicide of the senses and even of the self. It came from an eastern fanaticism like that of the fakirs and was ultimately founded on an eastern pessimism, which seems to feel existence itself as an evil.' Now, the most extraordinary thing about this is that it is not true of the Church; but it is true of the heretics condemned by the Church. (221–22)

Chesterton is always concerned with the inner world of the ascetic. He admits that Christianity had its desert dwellers and phenomenal feats of asceticism, but its inner world was different from that of the heretics: "The early Church was indeed very ascetic, in connection with a totally different philosophy; but the philosophy of a war on life and nature as such really did exist in the world, if only the critics knew where to look for it" (222). In the early centuries there really was

a sort of swarm of mystical and metaphysical sects. The difference was that only one golden dot in all that whirling gold-dust had the power of going forth to make hives for all humanity. The early Church was ascetic, but she proved that she was not pessimistic. The creed declared that man was sinful, but it did not declare that life was evil. They did not think life incurably miserable; they did not think marriage a sin or procreation a tragedy. They were ascetic because asceticism was the only possible purge of the sins of the world; but in the very thunder of their anathemas they affirmed forever that their asceticism was not to be anti-human or anti-natural; that they did wish to purge the world and not destroy it.

That the early Church was itself full of an ecstatic enthusiasm for renunciation and virginity makes this distinction much more striking and not less so. It makes all the more important the place where the dogma drew the line. A man might crawl about on all fours like a beast because he was an ascetic. He might stand night and day on the top of a pillar and be adored for being as ascetic. But he could not say that the world was a mistake or that the marriage state a sin without being a heretic. What was it that thus deliberately disengaged itself from eastern asceticism by sharp definition and fierce refusal, if it was not something with an individuality of its own; if it was not something quite different? It would be nearer the truth to call it [the Church] the tamer of asceticism than the mere leader or loosener of it. It was a thing having its own theory of asceticism, its own type of asceticism, but most conspicuous at the moment as the moderator of other theories and types. (223–25)

The "Escape From Paganism," as Chesterton called it (using the term as a chapter heading in *The Everlasting Man*), was an utterly unique escape from the prisons of all the mythologies and philosophies of the world, for it was not accomplished by a new mythology or a new philosophy. It can only be called a truly mystical event, the penetration of the world from the outside by the Presence: the Incarnation of God. In this sense Christianity is a mystical religion in its very essence, for by his absolute graciousness God revealed himself to our poor human race:

The moral of all this is an old one; that religion is revelation. In other words, it is a vision, and a vision received by faith; but it is a vision of reality. The faith consists in a conviction of its reality. (243)

When Chesterton accepted, by faith, the Incarnation of the Son of God, all the pieces of the human puzzle came together for him. It was the key. In other words, it was a mystical vision which illuminated all of reality for him: "There is something in the reasonable use of the very word vision that implies two things about it; first that it comes very rarely, possibly that it comes only once; and secondly that it probably comes once and for all" (243). Does this insight, "that it [the vision] probably comes once and for all," flow from his own experience?

Acceptance of the Incarnation brings together the two worlds in which the mystic ought to live:

The more deeply we think of the matter the more we shall conclude that, if there be indeed a God, his creation could hardly have reached any other culmination than this granting of a real romance to the world. Otherwise the two sides of the human mind could never have touched at all; and the brain of man would have remained cloven and double; one lobe of it dreaming impossible dreams and the other repeating invariable calculations. The picture-makers would have remained forever painting the portrait of nobody. The sages would have remained forever adding up numerals that came to nothing. It was that abyss that nothing but an incarnation could cover; a divine embodiment of our dreams.[5]

The Dividing Line

The Everlasting Man is a brilliant argument from history, showing the distinctiveness of Christianity, which is completely unlike all the other religions and philosophies. Just as people were saying in the nineteenth century that there really was not much difference between Christianity and other religions, between Christ and other great religious founders, so they were saying—and many are still saying this today—that *at the deepest level* there really are not any differences in the mystical experiences of people from various traditions. At bottom (the argument goes) all these experiences of the Presence are the same.

Not so, says Chesterton: "The religion of the world, in its right proportions, is not divided into fine shades of mysticism or more or less rational forms of mythology. It is divided by the line between the men who are bringing that message [of the Gospel] and the men who have not yet heard it, or cannot yet believe it" (267).

This is an important point to emphasize: not even all *authentic mysticisms are the same.* Although Chesterton deals mostly with true and false *ways* of envisioning reality, and not so much with

5 *The Everlasting Man,* 247. Cf. the end of *The Napoleon of Notting Hill,* where Chesterton describes each of the two main characters as representing one lobe of the brain.

the content of the mystic vision, his comment above about mysticism not being divided into "fine shades" merits a brief discussion at this point. I believe he would agree with the following conclusions. Stephen T. Katz is a world-recognized scholar in this area of comparative mysticism. He has written several books on the topic. I shall be referring to his article, "The Conservative Character of Mystical Experience."[6]

First of all, he emphasizes that there are no *pure*, unmediated religious experiences of the divine. (We would exempt Christ from this theory.) We have mystical experiences through the medium of who we are and what we think. These experiences, moreover, are conditioned by the religious and/or metaphysical concepts we have. As the scholastics used to say: "Whatever is received is received through the medium of the receiver." People do not have a pure, unfiltered experience of the Presence and then give it an interpretation. They have a *mediated* experience:

> What is argued is that, for example, the Hindu mystic does not have an experience of x which he describes in the, to him, familiar language and symbols of Hinduism, but rather he has a Hindu experience. Again, the Christian mystic does not experience some unidentified reality which he then conveniently labels 'God,' but rather has the at least partially prefigured Christian experiences of God. The Hindu experience of Brahman and the Christian experience of God are not the same. I stress how it is *experienced*, not merely how it is interpreted.[7]

I do not know enough about Chesterton's worldview at the time he had his early experiences of wonder at the *it-is-thereness* and the *goodness of being*. What did he believe about God and about the distinction between God and creatures at that stage of his life? Whatever it was, he had an experience according to his mode of perception at the time. It would be possible for him to have

6 Steven T. Katz (ed.), *Mysticism and Religious Traditions* (Oxford University Press, 1983), 3–60.
7 Ibid., 4–5, 13.

received, as a mystical grace, a sense of the wonder of being, without its having been a specifically Christian experience.

At that point in his journey Chesterton probably did not have a total Christian ontology with which to interpret his early experiences, since he only came across St. Thomas much later. But gradually he did arrive at it by discovering the key of Catholic orthodoxy. Here is Katz's broadly typical description of that Christian ontology:

> Christian mystics all presume an ontological skeleton which broadly approximates to this: there is a personal God who created (or emanated) the world. Men and women are his creation. The world and all else that is in it are his creation. The world and mankind are alienated from God as a result of original sin. A means of overcoming this alienation, however, has been provided by God through the mediation of Christ who is God incarnate, the second person of the Trinity. The human soul is capable of responding to this mediation because it is created by the Divine Being, incorporates the Divine, or is (depending on the technicalities of the different thinkers) Divine in itself. However, even the soul's divine origin is no guarantee of salvation unless God in his grace awakens the soul from its sensual this-worldly, imprisonment and turns it towards its maker and master.[8]

In the case of Chesterton, Katz's general description here must be qualified, tempered by the unique aspects of Chesterton's gift. It needs to be stressed that Chesterton's mystical grace was more precisely a reflexive turning towards the world in amazement, rather than a turning away from it. It was precisely a *this-worldly grace,* a celebration of the wonder and glory of material existence as reflecting the "immortally active" God. He experienced God *in the world.*

It is important to note here also that we are not talking about *moral differences* in the variety of mystical experiences. Only God knows who is really closer to him, the Hindu mystic or the Christian mystic. The grace of Christ can come to people in mysteri-

8 Ibid., 32–33.

ous ways, and the Church has never denied this. The point is that mystical experiences, because of the ontological perspectives of the mystic, are certainly not identical. And the theoretical conclusions and/or practical consequences of the various mystical experiences are certainly not identical either, nor guaranteed to be true. Hindu and Buddhist mystics draw very different conclusions about reality from their experiences.

Chesterton also has much to say about these different *effects* of the diverse views of reality. The burning, desert monotheism of Islam drives one to passionate extremes, and to an all-embracing, uncompromising religio-cultural unity. The Buddhist experience of *nirvana* has an inhibiting effect, conditioning a person to leave the world pretty much as it is. The Christian experience of the Trinity, however, if rightly understood, impels believers to strive for the unity of mankind and the socializing of the world in justice and truth.

But the main point here, to repeat, is that the mysticisms of the world are not the same; they are not on some sliding scale, different in degree, but not in kind, merely shading off into each another on one and same spectrum. Instead, a radically different ontology lies behind each of them. Once again Katz explains:

> Christian mystics have Christian experiences, of Jesus, Mary, and the mysteries of the Trinity, etc., while Jewish Kabbalists meet Elijah and 'see' the Merkabah or God's throne. In the East the Buddhists reach their goal, set by their ontology of anitya (impermanence) and suffering, of impersonal, stateless, attributeless, nirvana or satori, while Hindus confirm that Atman is Brahman, as they were taught from the onset of their mystical quest by the ruling metaphysical presuppositions of the Hindu schools.[9]

But even more significant for my purposes is Katz's main thesis:

> It is a commonplace of the study of mysticism to see it as the paradigm of religious individualism and radicalism. While it is true that mysticism contains elements of radical challenge

9 Ibid., 40.

to established religious authority and tradition, at the same time it embodies characteristics which are anything but radical.[10]

He says that the more common characteristics of mysticism are to "see the older tradition in a new guise; to give a personal confirmation of existing doctrine; to give a legitimate extension of traditional teaching, or a new but authoritative stage of tradition" (22). In short, authentic mysticism is deeply rooted in one's traditional religious tradition; it is, therefore, basically *conservative.*

In the following passage, Katz describes the basic practical thrusts of the mysticism of Teresa of Avila; what he says about her could be applied to Chesterton's mysticism as well. (Recall Chesterton's preference for the word "reform.")

> Her life's work was to renew the Church through her reform. Though the word 'reform' may conjure images of rebellion, associated most closely with Luther and the Protestant Reformation, it must be emphasized that reform is, at least in large measure, a fundamentally conservative factor which looks back to a real or imagined 'Golden Age' in some earlier, pristine period of a religious community's history. No religious reformer sees his or her self or work as essentially radical (i.e., novel or new), whatever the judgment of history may be. The thesis that mysticism has strong, if not dominant, conservative characteristics has at least begun to be demonstrated.[11]

Popularly we think of mystics as going "beyond all boundaries," having visions "beyond all concepts and structures," and thus, in practice, dispensing with the need for orthodox dogmas and/or religious structures. Katz's conclusions—which Chesterton saw decades ago—indicate that this is simply not so. The genuine mystics are deeply centered in their religious traditions. They enrich them from the inside by interiorizing and deepening them. By no means do they themselves disregard, or counsel oth-

10 Ibid., 36.
11 Ibid., 51.

ers to disregard, the ontological or traditional structures in which they themselves were formed.

In this sense, Chesterton's orthodoxy is a further argument for his having been a very genuine mystic. His mysticism did not propel him beyond doctrines and structures. It led him to the heart of orthodoxy. His mystical grace was rooted in humility and wisdom and openness to the truth. In due course, St. Francis and Thomas Aquinas served to broaden his Christian understanding of true mysticism by instructing him about "the form."

We have seen that, early in life, Chesterton enjoyed a real, immediate, grace-inspired experience of the Presence. (It is important to remember that the material of many of his books antedate, sometimes by years, the date of publication. And how long were the thoughts with him even before the first articles?) With the help of this grace he had come to basic truths which he later found confirmed in Christ's teachings. This is what I find in many of his early writings: that he was intuiting Gospel truths from within life itself, *"without much help from religion."* His faith in Christ raised these truths to higher dimensions; the Gospel revealed higher stakes. But many of the root truths of the Gospel about the nature of reality were already present in his experience.

Chesterton, early in life, had been amazed at the splendor of the humble dandelion. Christ in the Gospel pointed to the elegant clothing of the lilies of the field, and then related it to God's care for his children. Chesterton was already living in two worlds, but it was Christ who revealed to him the true nature of both. Many truths in the Gospel were not so much discovered as confirmed for him. Here is another example of what I mean:

'Take no thought what ye shall eat or what ye shall drink, or wherewithal ye shall be clothed. For after all these things do the Gentiles seek. But seek first the kingdom of God and His righteousness, and all these things shall be added unto you.' Those amazing words are not only extraordinarily good, practical politics; they are also superlatively good hygiene. The one supreme way of making all those processes go right, the processes of health, and strength, and grace, and beauty, the one and only way of making certain of their accuracy, is to think about something else.[12]

He will say later on in *Orthodoxy* that a healthy person does not think about his health. A person who plans to take a trip around the world must be very healthy indeed, or he would not be able to concentrate on planning such an enterprise, much less able to enjoy it. In such a case, good health is simply a given.

Applying this metaphor to the realm of the mystical, Chesterton is against people being preoccupied with an interior system of mysticism. If they are thus preoccupied, it often becomes a block to their ability to experience reality as it is. The interior world becomes a "mystification" which hinders true spontaneity and wonder: "For the thing called 'taking thought,' the thing for which the best modern word is 'rationalizing,' is in its nature, inapplicable to all plain and urgent things. Men take thought and ponder rationalistically, touching remote things—things that only theoretically matter, such as the transit to Venus. But only at their peril can men rationalize about so practical a matter as health."[13] He would certainly agree also that only at their peril do men rationalize about a mystical theory. It would be bad for their spiritual health.

In this matter we touch upon the notion of asceticism. The reader may be tempted to object: "All well and good for Chesterton to have a theory about the goodness of cigars and Burgundy and hackney cabs. He is just working out a theory to fit his tastes—and his weaknesses. Talk about a rationalization!"

Chesterton would be the first to admit his weaknesses in these areas. But he is fighting for a principle, for a way of relating to reality, for a way of being holy amidst material creation. He is concerned about the inside, the simplicity of the heart. This is more important than simplicity of life. He does not disparage the latter. He is not against (as we shall see) the asceticism of St. Francis, or of St. Simon Stylites, as long as such asceticism does not render them incapable of relating to real life with spontaneity

12 *Heretics*, 141.
13 Ibid.

and joy. He sums things up by saying, "Let us put a complex entree into a simple old gentleman; let us not put a simple entree into a complex old gentleman" (138).

He is concerned about false asceticism. Mr. Lowes Dickinson (cf. *Heretics*, Chapter XII) said that the big difference between paganism and Christianity was asceticism. With great emphasis, stating his disagreement in five different ways, Chesterton says it is not so:

> I take historic Christianity with all its sins upon its head, and I say that the meaning of its action was not to be found in asceticism. I say that its point of departure from Paganism was not asceticism. I say that its point of difference with the modern world was not asceticism. I say that St. Simeon Stylites had not his main inspiration in asceticism. I say that the main Christian impulse cannot be described as asceticism, even in the ascetics. (155)

I think he has made his point.

The principal difference, he asserts by way of rebuttal, is between the natural, pagan virtues of justice and temperance, which are sad and rational, and the mystical virtues of faith, hope, and charity, which are gay, exuberant, and "as unreasonable as they can be" (158). Chesterton found that the three mystical virtues of faith, hope, and charity were at the root of the simplicity of heart that protects the joy and exuberance of life from false asceticism. These three mystical and paradoxical virtues were exactly what he needed to live in elf land:

> As the word 'unreasonable' is open to misunderstanding, the matter may be more accurately put by saying that each one of these Christian or mystical virtues involves a paradox in its own nature.
>
> Charity means pardoning what is unpardonable, or it is no virtue at all. Hope means hoping when things are hopeless, or it is no virtue at all. And faith means believing the incredible, or it is no virtue at all.
>
> Charity is the power of defending that which we know to be indefensible. Hope is the power of being cheerful in cir-

cumstances which we know to be desperate. It is the unde-
serving who requires [charity], and the ideal either does not
exist at all, or exists wholly for them. For practical purposes
it is at the hopeless moment that we require the hopeful
man, and the virtue either does not exist at all, or begins to
exist at that moment. (158–59)

I find these insights into the Gospel from a lay journalist of Fleet
Street simply astounding. The clear, rational virtues stopped at
the borders of elf land. Paganism was really a world of common
sense. But when men came to the "stress of ultimate need, and a
terrible knowledge of things as they are" (161), new virtues were
needed; and Christianity gave birth to them:

Whatever may be the meaning of the contradiction, it is the
fact that the only kind of hope that is of any use in a battle is
a hope that denies arithmetic. Whatever may be the meaning of the contradiction, it is the fact that the only kind of
charity which any weak spirit wants, of which any generous
spirit feels, is the charity which forgives the sins that are like
scarlet. Whatever may be the meaning of faith, it must
always mean a certainty about something we cannot
prove. Thus, for instance, we believe by faith in the existence of other people. (162)

These are the mystical virtues necessary for Chesterton's vision
of reality. The neo-pagans of the modern world wish to go back
to reason and the sane, sad virtues of paganism; but we cannot.
They have proved insufficient for the human journey:

For mankind has discovered that reason does not lead to
sanity. Let [Mr. Lowes Dickinson] ignore these great historic
mysteries—the mystery of charity, the mystery of chivalry
[hope], the mystery of faith. But if we do revive and pursue
the pagan ideal of a simple and rational self-completion we
shall end—where Paganism ended. I do not mean that we
shall end in destruction. I mean that we shall end in Christianity. (170)

6

St. Francis:
Le Jongleur de Dieu

Chesterton loved St. Francis for most of his life. He had a statue of him in his parlor and paid him the tribute of his first book after his conversion to Catholicism in 1922.

Chesterton's discussion of the mysticism of St. Francis will serve to clarify, in a particular way, the true mystic's relationship to nature and the elements, exemplified so beautifully by his regard for Brother Sun and Sister Moon. As I hope to show, his book *St. Francis* will also expand our understanding of Chesterton's own mysticism. I submit that it is his most mystical book; especially the chapter entitled "Le Jongleur de Dieu." It is indeed so mystical, and in some ways so intellectually compact, that many people—myself included—miss a great deal of its profundity on first reading.

As an aid to understanding the book, I would like to attempt to unpack what it contains. If it is read with the optic of what I am saying about Chesterton's mysticism—that it is an intuition of the elemental and primary *"it-is-thereness* of being coming forth"—it makes more sense. From the point of view of ideas, it is as profound as anything you will read in Plotinus or any of the "intellectual mystics." Along with the mysticism of St. Thomas, which will be considered in the next chapter, it contains some of Chesterton's most profound thoughts about what he called, towards the end of his life, *"my original and almost mystical conviction."*

The Mystic as Tumbler

In the magnificent chapter, "Le Jongleur de Dieu," Chesterton gives some background on the troubadours in Provence and Languedoc, who influenced St. Francis. The Little Poor Man called his followers the "jongleurs de Dieu." Chesterton gives his interpretation of "jongleur":

> A jongleur was not the same thing as a troubadour, even if the same man were both a troubadour and a jongleur. The jongleur was properly a joculator or jester; sometimes he was what we should call a juggler. Sometimes he may have been a tumbler; like that acrobat in the beautiful legend who was called 'The Tumbler of Our Lady.' And when St. Francis called his followers the Jongleurs de Dieu, he meant something very like the Tumblers of Our Lady.[1]

Chesterton uses the image of tumbling, and of the mystic as a tumbler, to explain what happened to Francis: "There was, of course, a great more than this involved [in St. Francis's change of heart]; and we must endeavour however insufficiently to penetrate past the image to the idea. It is so far like the tumblers that it is really to many people a topsy-turvy idea" (101–102).

My contention is that the following description by Chesterton of what happened to Francis under the metaphor of tumbling could be applied to all genuine mystical experiences, his own included. Perhaps I should say that it stands as a description of what Chesterton would have *desired* to happen to all mystics. As we shall see shortly in reference to the Fraticelli, some "mystics" attempt their somersault, but do not land back on their feet; they land on their heads. And the stars created by such a fall blind them to the fullness of Catholic truth.

Happily, I am not concerned with whether or not this account of Chesterton's accurately describes the mysticism of St. Francis. It is frequently commented that Chesterton's writings about others are often very autobiographical. The question of whether Chesterton is faithfully describing Franciscan spirituality is the

---

1 *St. Francis*, 108–109. All page numbers in this chapter, unless otherwise noted, are from this book. As regards this first quote, Denis Conlon, in a private communication, said that, "GKC is not quite right in his definition. The jongleurs did sing the Chansons de geste and the Romans d'Aventures."

task of Franciscan scholars to sort out. What I have been delighted to discover is that this image describes the mysticism of Chesterton according to my theory! As always, the discerning reader will judge. In any case, when St. Francis landed back on his feet, he was a different man, and he saw the world—well, like Chesterton:

> Francis, at the time or somewhere about the time when he disappeared into the prison or the dark cavern, underwent a reversal of a certain psychological kind; which was really like the reversal of a complete somersault, in that by coming full circle it came back, or apparently came back, to the same normal posture. It is necessary to use the grotesque simile of an acrobatic antic, because there is hardly any other figure that will make the fact clear. But in the inward sense it was a profound spiritual revolution. (102)

This is one of Chesterton's key images for the mystical experience and its effects. It could be applied to anyone who has experienced a mystical touch from God. As I have been emphasizing, this touch can occur through almost any medium or any devotional act. It can occur anywhere— in a cave, in a prison, in the forest, before the Blessed Sacrament—or anytime.

The people we call mystics are those for whom such an experience endures as a more or less constant awareness, if not with the same intense tonalities as the original one, at least with the same depth of God-Presence which was communicated to them initially. And, most importantly of all, the *effects* of such an experience remain part of their permanent spiritual consciousness.

I am most concerned with these effects of the tumbling experience on Francis. They are similar to the same effects which formed part of Chesterton's own mystical awareness. Much of what he relates in *St. Francis* could be interpreted as a description of the effects, on him, of his own mystical tumbling:

> The man who went into the cave was not the man who came out again; in that sense he was almost as different as if he were dead, as if he were a ghost or a blessed spirit. And the effects of this on his attitude towards the actual world were

really as extravagant as any parallel can make them. He looked at the world as differently from other men as if he had come out of that dark hole walking on his hands. (102–03)

The "walking on his hands" is significant also, for later on Chesterton will use another related image for the mystical experience, that of seeing the world upside-down. What were some of the other effects caused by Francis's spiritual tumbling?

First of all, Francis did not enter the cave and stand on his head as a *technique in order to acquire a new experience.* "Our Lady's Tumbler did not stand on his head in order to see flowers and trees as a clearer or quainter vision. He did not do so; and it would never have occurred to him to do so. Our Lady's Tumbler stood on his head to please Our Lady" (104).

Part of the pseudo-mystical scene today involves the use of techniques *in order to achieve some kind of experience of God.* Francis's new vision occurred *after the fact* of seeking to please Our Lady. "That is why it is not true to represent St. Francis as a mere romantic forerunner of the Renaissance and a revival of natural pleasures for their own sake" (104). Francis's motive was "of a purely supernatural thought" (103). "The whole point of him was that the secret of recovering the natural pleasures lay in regarding them in the light of a supernatural pleasure" (104). From first to last, Francis's mysticism is bathed in a supernatural light, both in his original motives and as a background to his vision of reality.

A second effect of Francis's tumbling was the illumination of how *foolish he was:* "It was a solid objective fact like the stones in the road that he had made a fool of himself. And as he stared at the word 'fool' written in luminous letters before him, the word itself began to shine and change" (106). "When Francis came forth from his cave of vision, he was wearing the same word 'fool' as a feather in his cap; as a crest or even a crown. He would go on being a fool; he would become more and more of a fool; he would be the court fool of the King of Paradise" (107–08). We have from Francis's own lips the testimony that "the Lord asked me to be a fool the likes of which the world had never seen before."

Then Chesterton uses another image of the mystical experience which, again, could be applied to all such experiences. He recalls the story from the nursery about a man boring a hole through the center of the earth and going down so far that eventually he begins to come up. He says he has never done this himself and so cannot really verify it. Francis went so far down in humiliation that he came up in complete holiness or happiness. "It was so far analogous to the story of the man making a tunnel through the earth that it did mean a man going down and down until at some mysterious moment he begins to go up and up. We have never gone up like that because we have never gone down like that" (107).

I believe Chesterton did "go down like that," even though, in his humility, he says "of the intrinsic internal essence of the experience, I make no pretence of writing at all" (107). His whole vision of reality testifies to the fact that he did go down and down, and that he did come up and up. He was a humble man.

Another effect of the mystical tumbling, of seeing the world while standing on your head, is a profound experience of *dependence*, which is very closely allied to the virtue of *humility*, discovered by Chesterton very early in life:

'Humility,' as is well known, comes from the Latin word for earth, *humus*. You really do become humble after the mystical somersault, that is to say, 'grounded,' when you land back on the earth on your feet, but now with new eyes. In the upside-down phase of your mystic orbit, you see an extraordinary thing: the earth hanging. (109)

What Chesterton says, in the following quote about the town of Assisi, applies to every single creature, animate or inanimate, that God has made, and to every aspect of culture on the entire earth:

If a man saw the world upside down, with all the trees and towers hanging head downwards as in a pool, one effect would be to emphasize the idea of dependence. There is a Latin and literal connection; for the very word dependence only means hanging. It would make vivid the Scriptural text which says that God has hanged the world upon nothing. If

St. Francis had seen, in one of his strange dreams, the town of Assisi upside down, it need not have differed in a single detail from itself except in being entirely the other way round. But the point is this: that whereas to the normal eye the large masonry of its walls or the massive foundations of its watchtowers and its high citadel would make it seem safer and more permanent, the moment it was turned over the very same weight would make it seem more helpless and more in peril. It is but a symbol; but it happens to fit the psychological fact. St. Francis might love his little town as much as before, or more than before; but the nature of the love would be altered even in being increased. He might see and love every tile on the steep roofs or every bird on the battlements; but he would see them all in a new and divine light of eternal danger and dependence. Instead of being merely proud of his strong city because it could not be moved, he would be thankful to God Almighty that it had not been dropped; he would be thankful to God for not dropping the whole cosmos like a vast crystal to be shattered into falling stars. Perhaps St. Peter saw the world so, when he was crucified head-downwards. (108–09)

Chesterton is giving here some benchmarks for determining genuine mysticism. One sees the same things as before, but because of the "new and divine light," that is, the illuminative aspect of the mystical experience, one realizes everything's total dependence on God. One becomes humble when one realizes one's creaturehood, namely, that one is being upheld at each moment by a golden thread.

Experiencing this absolute dependence of everything on God, one receives a deep understanding of the true meaning of things:

It is also true that he sees more of the things themselves when he sees more of their origin; for their origin is a part of them and indeed the most important part. Thus they become more extraordinary by being explained. He has more wonder at them but less fear of them; for a thing is really wonderful when it is significant and not when it is insignificant; and a monster, shapeless or dumb or merely destructive, may be larger than the mountains, but it is still in a literal sense insignificant. For a mystic like St. Francis the monsters had a meaning; that is, they had delivered their message. They spoke no longer in an unknown tongue. That is the meaning of all those stories, whether legendary or historical, in which he appears as a magician speaking the language of beasts and birds. The mystic will have nothing to do with mere mystery; mere mystery is generally a mystery of iniquity. (110–11)

"Their origin is a part of them." What a profound insight! When we look upon creation we must realize that everything is dependent on God, is hanging upon his immortal creative activity. This is to see creation in its fullness of being by realizing that the origin of everything is part of its being.

The vision of everything depending upon God has another illuminative aspect. Mystically aware that Someone is holding everything up (or down), you see this Someone everywhere. Chesterton uses the difference between a poet and a mystic to define this distinction between ordinary and extraordinary consciousness. The following passage also describes the priority in Chesterton's mysticism of it-is-thereness over a secondary reflection on what is there:

The transition from the good man to the saint is a sort of revolution, by which one for whom all things illustrate and illuminate God becomes one for whom God illustrates and illuminates all things. It is rather like the reversal whereby a lover might say at first sight that a lady looked like a flower, and say afterwards that all flowers reminded him of his lady. (111)

A minor poet is once removed from reality, and may say that the sun is like a huge bonfire on the fourth of July. The saint and the mystic see primordial fire flaming forth emblematically from all of creation. Or, to draw closer to Chesterton's example, do you remember your first emotional, adolescent infatuation with someone, the glow of first love? For a time, anyhow, everyone is seen as an emanation of the beloved; everything is suffused and colored by the beloved, so that you can see nothing else. The beloved "illustrates and illumines all things," so to speak. Chesterton continues to elaborate this universal vision:

> A saint and a poet standing by the same flower might seem to say the same thing; but indeed though they would both be telling the truth, they would be telling different truths. For one the joy of life is a cause of faith, for the other rather a result of faith. (111)

It is important to see the crucial distinction he makes here, and its deep significance. What he is saying is that a direct intuition of the dependence of all things on God, a vivid appreciation that their origin derives from him, actually *causes* faith in the saint. The poet, on the other hand, who represents us ordinary mortals, has faith first and then sees God's presence in the flower.

Some clarifications are in order here.

Chesterton is not speaking here about the origins of *Christian faith*. Francis was a Christian before his divine tumbling, and most assuredly his faith in Christ and in his Father was an ingredient in his new mystical vision of the world. What Chesterton is talking about is a permanent way of seeing the world. For the poet the world is a kind of hazy background to individual things. Not so for the mystic. To get to the depth of this distinction, Chesterton utters what to many modern admirers of Francis may seem like a blasphemous statement by claiming that St. Francis was *not a lover of nature:*

> St. Francis was not a lover of nature. Properly understood, a lover of nature was precisely what he was not. The phrase implies accepting the material universe as a vague environment, a sort of sentimental pantheism. In the romantic period of literature, in the age of Byron and Scott, it was easy enough to imagine that a hermit in the ruins of a chapel (preferably by moonlight) might find peace and a mild pleasure in the harmony of solemn forests and silent stars, while he pondered over some scroll or illuminated volume, about the liturgical nature of which the author was a little vague. In short, the hermit might love nature as a background.

St. Francis: Le Jongleur de Dieu

Now for St. Francis nothing was ever in the background. We might say that his mind had no background, except perhaps that divine darkness out of which the divine love had called up every coloured creature one by one. In a word, we talk about a man who cannot see the wood for the trees. St. Francis was a man who did not want to see the wood for the trees. He wanted to see each tree as a separate and almost a sacred thing, being a child of God and therefore a brother or sister of man.

He is the very opposite of a pantheist. He did not call nature his mother; he called a particular donkey his brother or a particular sparrow his sister. If he had called a pelican his aunt or an elephant his uncle, as he might possibly have done, he would still have meant that they were particular creatures assigned by their Creator to particular places; not mere expressions of the evolutionary energy of things.

It was by this deliberate idea of starting from zero, from the dark nothingness of his own deserts, that he did come to enjoy even earthly things as few people have enjoyed them; and they are in themselves the best working example of the idea. (126–28)

When I was in Assisi in 1986 there were huge pictures of a polar bear on every post. An international environmental meeting was being held. St. Francis seems to have become nowadays the patron saint of lovers of the earth, the patron saint of Greenpeace. To be sure, I think Francis would have been delighted with Brother Bear's picture displayed all over his town. But my guess is that some of the people involved in this meeting would probably not see the origin of everything the way Francis did.

There is a "Gaia" doctrine current these days which holds that the world itself and everything in it is one immense living and breathing organism. There really is a great deal of sentimentality that underlies this whole trend of thought, as when animals, for instance, are proclaimed to have similar rights to those of humans. This is mawkish, sloppy thinking.

The next passage directly addresses some of these modern pantheists who, having lost a deeper, philosophical view of the nature of reality, lump it all together indiscriminately:

> That is where his mysticism is so close to the common sense of the child. A child has no difficulty about understanding that God made the dog and the cat; though he is well aware that the making of dogs and cats out of nothing is a mysterious process beyond his own imagination. But no child would understand what you meant if you mixed up the dog and the cat and everything else into one monster with myriad legs and called it nature.
>
> St. Francis was a mystic, but he believed in mysticism and not in mystification. As a mystic he was the mortal enemy of all those mystics who melt away the edges of things and dissolve an entity into its environment. He was a mystic of the daylight and the darkness; but not a mystic of the twilight. He was the very contrary of that sort of oriental visionary who is only a mystic because he is too much of a sceptic to be a materialist. (128–29)

Ready examples of this type of "oriental visionary" alluded to by Chesterton can be found in most forms of Hindu or Buddhist mysticism. Some of these systems actually do deny material reality: their adherents cannot land back on their feet after their mystical tumbling because there is nothing really to land on. They remain suspended in mid-air.

Chesterton calls them "mere mystics" or, in this case, "only mystics." These terms carry the same pejorative sense as the word "mystification." What he means (and we shall see a Christian instance of it when we come to the Fraticelli) is that these people have not yet come out of their somersaults. To repeat the images: they have landed jarringly on their heads instead of on their feet; or they have not gone down far enough into the divine darkness to start the journey back up. They have gone inward without coming out again to see the actual world with new eyes. They have not striven to acquire a correct appreciation of outward reality. Hence, they often have a distorted vision of truth. In Christian tradition we call such mystics—if their visions are too distorted—heresiarchs, and their obscure visions heresies.

In yet another profound paragraph Chesterton makes a very

subtle distinction between seeing things in their ever-present pristine origin from God—*"their origin is a part of them"*—and meeting them second-hand, as it were. Speaking again of the effects of mystical tumbling, he explains:

> But one effect of the difference is that the sense of a divine dependence, which for the artist is like the brilliant levin-blaze, for the saint is like the broad daylight. Being in some mystical sense on the other side of things, he sees things go forth from the divine as children going forth from a familiar and accepted home, instead of meeting them as they come out, as most of us do, upon the roads of the world. (III–12)

The genuine, saintly mystic, who has completed the somersault and landed back on his feet, is spiritually and psychologically *"on the other side of things."* His intuition of things coming forth from God is a constant daylight affair; he sees this all the time.

The poet, meanwhile, only gets lightning flashes (levin-blaze) once in a while. For the genuine mystic, created things are like children constantly coming forth from the creative being of God. As for us ordinary mortals, who are not in immediate touch with the emergent being of things, we wait on the road of life for them to reveal themselves at some special and privileged moments: "For us the elements are like heralds who tell us with trumpet and tabard that we are drawing near the city of a great king" (112).

In contrast, the mystic, on account of his immediate intuition of the origin of the elements at every moment, "is more familiar, freer and fraternal, more carelessly hospitable than we. He hails them with an old familiarity that is almost an old frivolity. He calls them his Brother Fire and his Sister Water" (112).

This intuition on the part of Francis—that he and all things are emerging at every moment from the same Father of all—is the source of a characteristic which Chesterton calls *courtesy*. Speaking of the time when Francis had his eyes cauterized, he says: "When they took the brand from the furnace, he rose as with an urbane gesture and spoke as to an invisible presence: 'Brother Fire, God made you beautiful and strong and useful; I pray you be courteous with me'" (137).

Francis's brotherhood was not of the back-slapping type, given to bluff, boisterous camaraderie: "That was not the equality which Francis of Assisi encouraged; but an equality of the opposite kind; it was a camaraderie actually founded on courtesy" (139).

> Even in that fairy borderland of his mere fancies about flowers and animals and even inanimate things, he retained this permanent posture of a sort of deference. A friend of mine said that somebody was the sort of man who apologises to the cat. St. Francis really would have apologised to the cat. When he was about to preach in a wood full of the chatter of birds, he said, with a gentle gesture, 'Little sisters, if you have now had your say, it is time that I also should be heard.' And all the birds were silent; as I for one can very easily believe. (139–40)

At every moment everything is actually proceeding from the abyss of the creativity of God. The mystic has entered this abyss and returned from it through his spiritual tumbling.

This abyss is so dreadful and formidable, so utterly fathomless, that Chesterton makes bold, in the following passage, to call it an *"almost nihilistic abyss."* The following is one of the best and most moving explications of Chesterton's own mysticism, a striking keynote of which is *praise*:

> So arises out of this almost nihilistic abyss the noble thing that is called Praise; which no one will ever understand while he identifies it with nature-worship or pantheistic optimism. When we say that a poet praises the whole of creation, we commonly mean only that he praises the whole cosmos. But this sort of poet [the mystic] does really praise creation, in the sense of the act of creation. He praises the passage or transition from nonentity to entity.
>
> The mystic who passes through the moment when there is nothing but God does in some sense behold the beginningless beginnings in which there was really nothing else. He not only appreciates everything but the nothing of which everything was made. In a fashion he endures and answers

even the earthquake irony of the Book of Job; in some sense
he is there when the foundations of the world are laid, with
the morning stars singing together and the sons of God
shouting for joy. (112–13)

In this exquisitely mystical language we have a superb overview
of Chesterton's mysticism. Quite evident is his constant intuition
of the amazing *it-is-thereness of being*. Equally, he is very much
aware that at every moment creatures are originating from God.
Since every moment is witness to the action of God's creating
power, it is no mere hyperbole to say that the true mystic is ever
present at the very foundations of the world. What is more, he
even appreciates "*the nothing of which everything was made.*"

I would like to make a comment about the following two
phrases that occur in this passage: "the beginningless beginnings
in which there was really nothing else," and "the nothing of
which everything was made."

I prefer Chesterton's first phrase; the second is the traditional
one about God making things out of nothing. But, actually, *nothing doesn't exist*. What we mean when we say "out of nothing" is
that at one time, in the aeons of God's eternity, there was only
God. While there was nothing created (unless one believes in the
eternity of created beings outside of God, which Aquinas said
was philosophically tenable), still, everything was *filled with God*.
Chesterton's phrase "the beginningless beginnings in which
there was really nothing else" means "the beginingless beginnings in which there was nothing else *except God*."

His mysticism consists of being aware that at every moment,
and not just "in the beginning," God is creating and suspending
everything by his creative act. This intuitive awareness that all is
hanging on his power and proceeding from his pure graciousness
lies at the source of Chesterton's mysticism. An even more exact
way of describing his mystical grace would be this: a mystical
awareness of the *thereness-of-being coming forth*. How much his
mysticism overlaps with that of St. Francis is another question.
Whatever the case, the immediacy and vigor of his sense of mystic dependence arise obviously from the fruits of his own passionate experience of the Presence:

This sense of the great gratitude and the sublime dependence was not a phrase or even a sentiment; it is the whole point that this was the very rock of reality. It was not a fancy but a fact; rather it is true that beside it all facts are fancies. That we all depend in every detail, at every moment, as even an agnostic would say, upon existence and the nature of things, is not an illusion of imagination; on the contrary, it is the fundamental fact which we cover up, as with curtains, with the illusion of ordinary life. That ordinary life is an admirable thing in itself, just as imagination is an admirable thing in itself. But it is much more the ordinary life that is made up of imagination than the contemplative life. He who has seen the whole world hanging on a hair of the mercy of God has seen the truth; we might almost say the cold truth. He who has seen the vision of his city upside-down has seen it the right way up. (113–14)

By "the contemplative life" I understand him to mean the presence of an interior vision, enabling a person to gain some notion of "the whole world hanging on a hair of the mercy of God." Everyday consciousness, on the other hand, uses the imagination to cover up with the illusion of ordinary life, the illusion of the deists that everything was created long ago and is now simply "lasting" like a machine running down. No, everything at every moment is coming forth from God. To live with the abiding consciousness of the truth that creation depends on God is to be filled, he says, with gratitude: "The great painter boasted that he mixed all his colours with brains, and the great saint may be said to mix all his thoughts with thanks. All goods look better when they look like gifts" (114).

But lying even deeper than seeing everything as akin to a birthday present is the realization that we are *in debt*: "The shortest statement of one aspect of this illumination is to say that it is the discovery of an infinite debt."

To be debtors to the Lord is not a new idea. We read in St. Paul: "Therefore, brothers, we have an obligation, but it is not to the sinful nature" (Rom. 8:12). Older translations say, "we are *debtors*," rather than "we have an obligation." In the Latin rendering of the

Bible, this passage is translated by recourse to the word *debitores*, which echoes the exact meaning of the Greek term in the original text. The singular of *debitores* is *debitor*, which means: "a debtor, one who owes, one who is indebted."

Perhaps modern people have too many unpleasant experiences of owing money to the banks or credit card companies, which makes "having an obligation" a less painful translation. In any case, Chesterton thinks being in debt *to* God (which is what St. Paul implies in the rest of that passage) can be a joyful experience, flowing from the intuition that we all hang on God's boundless love and creativity:

> It may seem a paradox to say that a man may be transported with joy to discover that he is in debt. But this is only because in commercial cases the creditor does not generally share the transports of joy; especially when the debt is by hypothesis infinite and therefore unrecoverable. But here again the parallel of a natural love-story of the nobler sort disposes of the difficulty in a flash. There the infinite creditor does share the joy of the infinite debtor; for indeed they are both debtors and both creditors. In other words debt and dependence do become pleasures in the presence of unspoilt love; the word is used too loosely and luxuriously in popular simplifications like the present; but here the word is really key. (116–17)

The Key to Asceticism

When, earlier in this chapter, Chesterton was quoted as saying that St. Peter saw the world upside-down when he was crucified, he did not elaborate on the subject of suffering and asceticism. Certainly St. Peter was suffering then, as he looked out on the world from this fresh, new perspective. It is, indeed, quite possible for an initial mystical experience to be all joy and light and bliss, but not necessarily so. In the main, however, it must be said that there is an ascetical, purifying dimension which is absolutely essential in sustaining the new view of reality that results from the tumbling. As Chesterton points out, the mystical experience drives one towards asceticism for principally two reasons: as an attempt to pay the unpayable debt; and as a means to keep God as the absolutely first love in one's life among all our other loves:

> It [being in debt] is the key of all the problems of Franciscan morality which puzzle the merely modern mind; but above all it is the key of asceticism. It is the highest and holiest of the paradoxes that the man who really knows he cannot pay his debt will be forever paying it. He will be forever giving back what he cannot give back, and cannot be expected to give back. He will be always throwing things away into a bottomless pit of unfathomable thanks. (117)
>
> He was above all things a great giver; and he cared chiefly for the best kind of giving which is called thanksgiving. If another great man wrote a grammar of assent [Newman], he may well be said to have written a grammar of acceptance; a grammar of gratitude. He understood down to its very depths the theory of thanks; and its depths are a bottomless abyss. He knew that the praise of God stands on its strongest ground when it stands on nothing. He knew that we can best measure the towering miracle of the mere fact of existence if we realise that but for some strange mercy we should not even exist. (230–31)

George MacDonald, whom both Chesterton and C.S. Lewis acknowledged as their teacher in story telling (cf. Chapter 8), has one of his Christ-figures say, "Well, you know, God is easy to please but hard to satisfy."

In spiritual direction, I often quote this to people if I think they are too scrupulous, or trying to satisfy, in an impossible way, some demanding, taskmaster image of God. I tell them that the slightest act of love pleases the Lord.

But the saints are not satisfied with this. They know God's love is insatiable, that the debt is unpayable—but they try to repay it all the same. Their immense love seeks to repay love for love. Impossible, of course, but loves does such things:

> Men who think they are too modern to understand this [forever paying an unpayable debt] are in fact too mean to

understand it; we are most of us too mean to practise it. We are not generous enough to be ascetics; one might almost say not genial enough to be ascetics. A man must have magnanimity of surrender, of which he commonly only catches a glimpse in first love, like a glimpse of our lost Eden. But whether he sees it or not, the truth is in that riddle; that the whole world has, or is, only one good thing; and it is a bad debt. (117)

Chesterton calls this magnanimous attitude "romantic love," and suggests that, if we ever lose it, we will have lost chivalry in love just as we have lost chivalry in war. "They will have lost the clue to all that lovers have meant by love; and will not understand that it is because a thing was not demanded that it was done" (118).

He says that because some *have* lost this key to love, they cannot understand the asceticism of the saints. They call it gloomy. And I have often heard people call asceticism masochistic, sadistic, and other such pejorative terms. It certainly *can* be that; indeed, it *might have been that* in some of the "mere mystics." But not so in Francis, not so in the real mystics:

> The whole point about St. Francis of Assisi is that he certainly was ascetical and he certainly was not gloomy. As soon as ever he had been unhorsed by the glorious humiliation of his vision of dependence on the divine love, he flung himself into fasting and vigil exactly as he had flung himself furiously into battle. He wheeled his charger clean round, but there was no halt or check in the thundering impetuosity of his charge. There was nothing negative about it; it was not a regimen or a stoical simplicity of life. It was not self-denial merely in the sense of self-control. It was as positive as a passion; it had all the air of being as positive as a pleasure. (119)

A further reason, therefore, for what is variously called detachment or ascetical distance from things and relationships lies in the glorious humiliation that comes with the vision of dependence on the divine love, which is linked, of course, to the intuitive sense that everything hangs on God's creative action at every moment.

Saints are often said to be "detached." This distance can often cause others to perceive them as impersonal or not fully human. Yet the reason is simply that the vision of the divine Presence has put everything into proper perspective, and the mystics must strive to keep it that way. If they are really immersed in God, they need to order their lives in such a way that they can continue to experience everything in relationship to him:

> It is certain that the mystical method establishes a very healthy external relation to everything else. But it must always be remembered that everything else has forever fallen into a second place, in comparison with this simple fact of dependence on the divine reality. In so far as ordinary social relations have in them something that seems solid and self-supporting, some sense of being at once buttressed and cushioned; in so far as they establish sanity in the sense of security and security in the sense of self-sufficiency, the man who has seen the world hanging on a hair does have some difficulty in taking them so seriously as that. (115)

What wonderfully deep spirituality! All of us struggle with the tension between loving God and loving neighbor. The problem lies in keeping these loves in proper order. Saints can sometimes strike us as distant and impersonal because they have experienced their absolute dependence on God, and are not seeking to rest in human relationships. They can no longer "take them too seriously."

This deep spirituality brings about a similar lack of seriousness in relation to social structures and in relation to our very selves:

> In so far as even the secular authorities and hierarchies, even the most natural superiorities and the most necessary subordinations, tend at once to put a man in his place, and to make him sure of his position, the man who has seen the human hierarchy upside down will always have something of a smile for its superiorities. In this sense the direct vision of divine reality does disturb solemnities that are sane enough in themselves. (115)

St. Francis: Le Jongleur de Dieu

People often refer to an experience of the divine reality as a new birth. St. Paul speaks of being a new man in Christ. Such experiences often give one a totally different view of oneself:

> The mystic may have added a cubit to his stature; but he generally loses something of his status. He can no longer take himself for granted, merely because he can verify his own existence in a parish register or a family Bible. Such a man may have something of the appearance of the lunatic who has lost his name while preserving his nature; who straightaway forgets what manner of man he was 'Hitherto I have been called Pietro Bernadone, father; but now I am the servant of God.' (115–16)

7

St. Thomas:
The Mystical Mind

One of the aspects of Chesterton's life and thought which eventually led me to ask about his mysticism was what I call his "charism of truth." Many observations about Chesterton center on the truth-quality of his mind. In 1986, Cardinal Carter of Toronto, commenting in his homily at the Chesterton Anniversary Conference Mass, mentioned Chesterton's "truly prophetic gift." Writing from England, J.J. Scarisbrick wrote in response:

> We all know that he was an enormously good man as well as enormous man. Above all, there was that breathtaking, intuitive (almost angelic) possession of the Truth and awareness of the supernatural which only a truly holy person can enjoy. This was the gift of heroic intelligence and understanding—and of heroic prophecy. He was a giant spiritually as well as physically. Has there ever been anyone quite like him in Catholic history?[1]

Chesterton's mysticism reveals itself most especially in the realm of the mind. People often know very little about him personally, but they are drawn to him by the depth of his insights. Some of the Church's great minds such as Origen, Augustine and Aquinas have spoken with such depth that the Church has concluded that they were close to God. Would they have been canonized if they had not written those profound things? To be canonized one must have lived the Gospel to a heroic degree.

---

1 *The Chesterton Review,* November 1986, 564.

St. Thomas: The Mystical Mind

Can this heroic virtue be manifested and authenticated through the Gospel quality of one's mind? The Church answers yes.

Before considering the questions of whether or not the use of the intellect is a hindrance to mysticism (Chesterton used his mind very much), and the difference between the mysticism of Thomas and Francis, I begin with some comments on the purification of the intellect according to one of the most prominent of modern Thomists, Reginald Garrigou-Lagrange, O.P., in his *Three Ages of the Interior Life*.[2] Chesterton had some kind of purified mind.

For me, the attractiveness of Chesterton is not only in the profound truth of *what* he says, but in the very qualities of his mind. Loving St. Thomas as he did, Chesterton wouldn't mind if I use Thomistic terms to define what the Holy Spirit had achieved in him: the active purification of the intellect through the *gift of knowledge*.

Since original sin (the only doctrine, Chesterton remarks, which needs no proof), our intellect is wounded as well as our other bodily powers. The most comprehensive name for this particular wound of the mind is ignorance. With the help of Lagrange, let me first list the various aspects of this ignorance, and then briefly comment on how the qualities of Chesterton's mind exemplifies the healing of these wounds.

The defects of the mind which exist in us in various degrees are: curiosity, rash haste to learn what is useless, indifference, negligence in regard to the one thing necessary (i.e., God and our salvation), spiritual pride, blindness, and spiritual folly. These defects incite us to judge everything by what is lowest and most petty, whereas wisdom judges everything in the light of the supreme cause and our last end (359).

Original sin has not destroyed our ability to know the truth, but it has weakened our ability to discover the truth. Our prideful passions obscure our minds and darken its comprehension and search for truth. Chesterton's mind portrays many aspects of its purification by the Holy Spirit's *gift of knowledge*.

2 (St. Louis: B. Herder Book Co., 1957). Page references in this section refer to this book unless otherwise noted.

Let us begin with the sin of curiosity, "which inclines us with eagerness and precipitation toward the consideration and study of less useful subjects, making us neglect the things of God and our salvation" (354).

I've seen something of Chesterton's personal library. I believe he read books on every conceivable subject. I recall the incident when he was looking for his shoe under the bed, found a book there, and remained for an hour or so reading in that quite comfortable and private place. Isn't this "curiosity"?

I think not. One gets the impression he was precisely reading everything in order to harmonize everything of human culture into his faith vision. He passion for knowledge was akin to that of St. Albert the Great, the teacher of Aquinas who, in order to glorify God, acquired an encyclopedic knowledge of the world of his day.

Chesterton's breadth of knowledge did not retard his vision of the faith, or make him slothful in reading more sublime topics. The sin of curiosity stores "useless knowledge which does not at all form the judgment"; it is a "mania for collecting, an accumulation of knowledge mechanically arranged and unorganized, somewhat as if it were in a dictionary"; it is "a jumble of accumulated knowledge, [unable] to see the light of the first principles" (355). When Chesterton, in the bath tub, read a stack of books on a certain topic prior to his own unique creation, what emerged from this immersion was not a compendium of all he had read, but a distillation related to the highest principles in a most poetic way. He was precisely devouring knowledge in order to relate it to the "one thing necessary."

St. Thomas's commentary on Paul's "knowledge puffeth up," fits our hero:

> Here the Apostle does not approve of much knowledge, if the mode of knowing is ignored. Moreover, the mode of knowing is that you should know in what order, with what eagerness, to what end each thing must be known: in what order, that you should know first that which is more proper for salvation; with what eagerness, that you should seek with greater ardor that which is more efficacious to inflame love; to what end, that you should not wish to know any-

thing for vainglory and curiosity, but for your own and your neighbor's edification. (355)

"Vainglory" brings us to spiritual pride.

Spiritual pride is a more serious disorder than curiosity. It gives us such confidence in our own reason and judgment that we are not very willing to enlighten ourselves by the benevolent and attentive examination of reasons or facts which may be urged against us. It leads also to asperity in discussion, to stubbornness in judgment, to disparagement which excludes in a cutting tone all that does not fit in with our manner of seeing things. This pride may lead a person to refuse to others the liberty he claims for his own opinions (356).

There are so many things about Chesterton which delight me, but near the top of my list is this intellectual graciousness with which he approaches his intellectual foes, a graciousness which witnesses to his intellectual humility as well as to his charity for the misguided and deluded.

I don't have quotes handy, and I will not attempt to quote from memory as Chesterton mostly did. I will not presume to quote, but audaciously compose a very typical opening salvo which Chesterton might have used in refuting his adversaries. (We could learn much from him these days in our often acrimonious Catholic debates.)

I have just finished reading a very stimulating and far-ranging article on the origin of *homo sapiens* by the distinguished author Mr. Cornelius McGillicuddy. I certainly defend his right to expose his mind to public view. My only comment would be that if the contents of his mind are further poured forth upon us, the results would truly be most disastrous for the future of *homo sapiens*.

Or that famous passage where Mr. So and So is decrying the fact that the early Christians allowed themselves to be eaten by the lions. They only needed to make some kind of mental reservation to spare themselves from such an ordeal. Chesterton comments that Mr. So and So is the only Christian, in his opinion, that really ought to be fed to the lions!

You can't help but really believe that each of these opponents would have enjoyed going out afterwards with Chesterton to a pub to continue the discussion. He was open to the opinions of others, and respected and loved them as persons. He often thought, however, that their ideas were disastrous. Spiritual pride can lead to spiritual blindness, where knowledge blocks out the voice of God. "Blind guides," Jesus called some of the learned of his day.

> We may say of [spiritual blindness] what St. Thomas says of spiritual folly (*stultitia*), that it is opposed to the precepts of the contemplation of truth, a tendency that is, so to speak, anti-contemplative, permitting them to see the life of the Church only from without, as if they were looking at the exterior of the windows of a cathedral, instead of seeing them from within under the soft light which should illumine them. (357–58)

Chesterton had a charitable mind, subject to faith, distinguishing between the person and his ideas. Great medievalist that he was, he was an outstanding example of what the greatest contemplative of the Middle Ages, St. Bernard, said:

> There are those who wish to know, for the purpose of knowing a great deal, and this is curiosity; some that they may know, and this is vanity; some that they may sell their knowledge, and this is base gain; some that they may be edified, and this is prudence; some that they may edify, and this is charity. (362)

The Gift of Knowledge

Chesterton's wife Frances once asked him why he didn't write more about God. He replied, "I am always writing about God." But his gift was not that of theological wisdom properly so-called, writing explicitly about the mysteries of the faith. His was the gift of a sort of sacred practical theology, to treat of human affairs in the light of faith. He wrote of St. Francis: "[He] cast a new supernatural light on natural things, the ultimate recovery, not refusal, of natural things." That's an exact definition of the gift Chesterton had through his mystical grace. St. Augustine called this the *gift of knowledge*:

> St. Augustine: According to the distinction which the apostle made when he said, 'to one is given the word of wisdom, to another the word of knowledge,' that definition must be divided: the knowledge of divine things is properly wisdom, and that of human things is properly called knowledge. It is one thing to know only what a man ought to believe in order to attain to a blessed life, which is none other than eternal life; and another to know how this may be of assistance to the pious, and be defended against the wicked, what the apostle seems to call by the special designation of knowledge.[3]

This grace of immediacy with the Presence gave a certain definite quality to his thinking. The grace of "knowledge of divine things, wisdom" impelled Aquinas, for example, to sit down quietly and contemplate the large, eternal plan of things. Chesterton's grace riveted him on present realities, that which journalists are interested in: "I have no feeling for immortality. I don't care for anything except to be in the present stress of life as it is. I would rather live now and die, from an artistic point of view, than keep aloof and write things that will remain in the world hundreds of years after my death."[4]

Chesterton's gift was "to know how [the eternal truths] may be of assistance to the pious, and be defended against the wicked." And, in spite of his wish not to remain in the world a hundred years after his death, his writings have withstood the test of time extremely well. (As of this writing, we only have 23 more years to go before 2036!) This "test of time" is another proof of the profundity of his grace. Although he was immersed

---

3 Benedict XIV, Pope. *Heroic Virtue: A Portion of the Treatise of Benedict XIV on the Beatification and Canonization of the Servants of God.* Trans. by the English Fathers of the Oratory (London: Thomas Richardson and Son, 1850), 104–105.

4 Quoted by Aidan Mackey in "Chesterton, Fidei Defensor," *30 Days*, October, 1989.

in the issues of his day, his insights have a lasting value. This does not mean, of course, that he was right about everything; but he was right about most things.

I don't know about the present reader, but when I read Chesterton I find myself saying, "It's true. It's true." Chesterton said that the Church was a *"truth-telling Thing."* Chesterton was a truth-telling mystic.

Do Mystics Study and Use Their Minds?

There is a disputed question as to the place of study in the mystical quest which is relevant to our discussion of whether Chesterton was a mystic or not. Don't mystics turn their minds off and remain in the darkness of faith? Some do, and some don't. While St. Francis saw dangers in the use of the mind, St. Thomas saw dangers only in how to use it. Thomas did not doubt that the mind should be used.

It is a matter of debate among the schools of mysticism whether or not learning and study should have a place in the mystical, contemplative life. There is one ancient and strong tradition which says that books, learning, and study are not only unnecessary for the deeper life with God, but positively an obstacle. It would be very easy to marshal hundreds of quotations from the desert fathers, from the monks (especially from the East), and from the writings of some of the mystics, to the effect that learning is an obstacle to the final ascent of the spirit to God. All that is necessary is the Holy Scriptures. For the rest, the mind should be free from the interference of intellectual activity, as it seeks to live entirely by the inspirations of the Holy Spirit:

> As oft I say 'all the creatures that ever be made' are [to be eliminated], so oft do I mean, not only the creatures themselves, but also all the works and conditions of the same creatures. I except not one creature, whether they be bodily creatures or ghostly; good or evil. But, so speak shortly, all should be hid under the cloud of forgetting in this case.[5]

5 *The Cloud of Unknowing*, Dom Justin McCann (ed.), (London: Burns & Oates, 1943), 11–12.

Although this text does not specifically mention study, the presupposition is that the heights of contemplation do not admit of rational thinking about any creatures. When the mind is in use, contemplation is imperfect. How can Chesterton be a mystic if he didn't stop his mind and enter the cloud of unknowing?

However, there is definitely another even stronger tradition—Irenaeus, Justin, Origen, the Cappadocians, Augustine, Jerome, Maximus the Confessor, Aquinas, Anselm and countless other Fathers. Many or most of these great Fathers were certainly mystics. They, of course, knew of the tradition of giving up the use of one's mind in order to "know God better," but they evidently disagreed: their vast literary output showed that they had no difficulty with the intellectual life as such. For them it was a matter of how to use the mind, not whether or not to use it. Their libraries were often enormous, and study did not lessen their union with God. They believed, of course, that all knowledge had to be subject to the light of Christ. "All truth comes from the Holy Spirit," was a common patristic saying, but they did not see knowledge per se as hindering the mystical life.

Chesterton has a brief section on this subject in *St. Francis*. As is well known, Francis was not all that enthusiastic about books. He himself wrote: "Let the illiterate not worry about learning to read, but consider that above all things they should desire to have the spirit of the Lord and its holy working."[6]

> The truth would seem to be that, although not categorically opposed to learned study by the friars, he had the gravest reservations about it, for the good reason that it was a threat to all four prime characteristics of Franciscan life—poverty, humility, simplicity, the spirit of devotion.[7]

It's interesting to see how Chesterton handles this topic in relation to Francis. Basically he says that Francis was unique, and that as the one who stands at the origin of the medieval age, it was not necessary for him to know what went before:

6 Duncan Nimmo, *Reform and Division in the Franciscan Order* (Rome: Capuchin Historical Institute, 1987), 22.
7 Ibid.

There is not a trace in the poetry of this first Italian poet of all that pagan mythology which lingered after paganism. The first Italian poet seems the only man in the world who has never even heard of Virgil. This was exactly right for the special sense in which he is the first Italian poet. It is the essence of the story that he should pluck at the green grass without knowing it grows over a murdered man or climb the apple tree without knowing it was the gibbet of a suicide. It was such an amnesty and reconciliation that the freshness of the Franciscan brought to all the world.[8]

But Chesterton is very grateful that the Fraticelli, who would have turned this grace of Francis into a principle, did not prevail. He is glad Dante knew of Virgil; glad, too, that the Franciscans produced Bonaventure, Raymond Lull, Roger Bacon, and Duns Scotus.

It is not merely true that these were great men who did great work for the world; it is also true that they were a certain kind of men keeping the spirit and savour of a certain kind of man, that we can recognise in them a taste and tang of audacity and simplicity, and know them for the sons of St. Francis.[9]

Chesterton's voracious appetite for knowledge, therefore, is not opposed to authentic mysticism: his vocation required it. He had the gift of knowledge, which precisely is reflection on the practical aspects of life in order to illumine them with the light of faith. One needs open eyes for this task. He did not see the things of earth as distracting him from a mystical vision of the Presence. His experience of the Presence was mediated precisely through the stimuli which the five windows of his nature could afford him.

Similarly, he experienced the Presence, as St. Thomas did, in the truths his mind was able to assimilate, for God is Truth as well as Love. We commonly and frequently say that if you love, you touch God, since God is Love. It also follows that, if God is

8 *St. Francis*, 225–226.
9 Ibid., 230.

Truth, when your mind knows truth, you are also, in a real sense, touching God, the First Truth. It was this "First Truth" Who often communicated with St. Catherine of Siena:

Then Eternal Truth seized her desire and drew it more strongly to himself. She lifted up her spirit and gazed into eternal Truth with her mind's eye. 'I am certain, eternal Truth, that you will not spurn my desire and the petitions I have addressed to you.' The First Truth showed her; then the Eternal Truth seized and drew more strongly to Himself her desire; the Sweet Truth continued.[10]

Coming, as this does, from one of the great mystics of the Middle Ages, this is an inspired corroboration of an attitude towards the gift of the mind which many learned Christian Fathers and teachers possessed.

St. Thomas: "Taste and See"

Thomas Aquinas—the mystical mind—completes Chesterton's Christian understanding of mysticism.

It is hard to say exactly when Chesterton first heard of Aquinas (there is a reference to him in *Heretics*), or really seriously studied him. We do, however, know that his brilliant, book-length study of Saint Thomas Aquinas appeared late in his life, three years before his death in 1936.[11] Nor is it easy to say where or when he conceived his exalted notion of Aristotle, whom he called the wisest and greatest mind that ever existed (cf. *The Everlasting Man*). Whatever the case, in both Thomas Aquinas and Aristotle he found the philosophical position which explained his own mystical intuition of Being. Aquinas is the philosopher of *ens*, of the *it-is-thereness* of being. And Chesterton is the mystic of the *thereness-of-being coming forth*. The Presence was manifested most of all in being constantly issuing forth from the good God.

In the chapter in St. Thomas entitled "The Aristotelian Revolu-

10 Catherine of Siena, *The Dialogue* (New York: Paulist Press, 1980), 202–204.
11 (London: Hodder & Stoughton, 1933). Page references in this section refer to this book unless otherwise noted.

tion," Chesterton has the following description of St. Bonaventure, the great Franciscan theologian of the Middle Ages:

> The Franciscan may be represented as the Father of all the Mystics; and the Mystics can be represented as men who maintain that the final fruition or joy of the soul is rather a sensation than a thought. The motto of the Mystics has always been, 'Taste and see.' (73)

In mentioning "final fruition" Chesterton is referring briefly to the interminable question of which has ultimate finality, love or knowledge. The question is not of immediate concern to us here, although it must be said that Chesterton does come down gently on the side of knowledge: "The appetite for truth may outlast and even devour all the duller appetites of man" (74). My main concern is this other statement that occurs in the same context, where Chesterton compares St. Thomas, the Dominican, with St. Bonaventure, the Franciscan:

> The motto of the Mystics has always been, 'Taste and see.' Now St. Thomas also began by saying, 'Taste and see'; but he said it of the first rudimentary impressions of the human animal. It might well be maintained that the Franciscan puts taste last and the Dominican puts it first. It might be said that the Thomist begins with something solid like the taste of an apple, and afterwards deduces a divine life for the intellect; while the Mystic exhausts the intellect first, and says finally that the sense of God is something like the taste of an apple. (73)

What does Chesterton mean when he refers to Bonaventure as a mystic, in seeming contrast to Thomas? Indeed, he calls Bonaventure the "Father of all the mystics." I'm sure he considered Thomas a mystic no less than he did Bonaventure. When he uses the term "mystics" here, he is speaking about the more broadly accepted definition of mysticism, about people who devise elaborate theories about the Presence behind sensible reality. In this vein, for example, many consider Plato a genuine mystic who "exhausted the intellect" in profound speculations about the nature of things, and then concluded that a sense of the presence of God can be "tasted": rays and vestiges of the Presence can be seen or experienced in our tangible world. Both Aquinas and Chesterton contend that human consciousness begins with the taste of the intuition of being:

> St. Thomas says emphatically that the child is aware of Ens. Long before he knows that grass is grass, or self is self, he knows that something is something. Perhaps it would be best to say very emphatically (with a blow on the table), 'There is an Is.' That is as much monkish credulity as St. Thomas asks of us to believe at the start. (166)

Thomas and Chesterton begin their journey with the extraordinariness of *ens* itself. They believe we first "taste," with the totality of our faculties, the elementary existence of things, and "see" afterwards. Their mysticism is not a reposing "in the peace of timeless being," in the interior vision, but in the actual tasting of reality. My contention is that Chesterton's intuition went beyond simple awareness of being: for him it was the *thereness-of-being coming forth*.

In summing up the essence of Thomism, Chesterton says:

> He [Aquinas] is arguing for the popular proverbs that seeing is believing; that the proof of the pudding is in the eating; that a man cannot jump down his own throat or deny the fact of his own existence. (156)

We have seen that "mere mystic" is another tag Chesterton uses for mystics who are more fascinated by the inner world they construct than by the amazing world they can see:

> 'Everything that is in the intellect has been in the senses.' This is where he began at the opposite end of enquiry from that of the mere mystic. The Platonists, or at least the Neo-Platonists, all tended to the view that the mind was lit entirely from within; St. Thomas insisted that it was lit by five windows, that we call the windows of the senses. But he wanted the light from without to shine on what was within. (161)

Man is not a balloon going up into the sky, nor a mole

burrowing merely in the earth; but rather a thing like a tree, whose roots are fed from the earth, while its highest branches seem to rise almost to the stars. (164)

In the last paragraph of the chapter entitled, "The Permanent Philosophy," Chesterton tries to sum up St. Thomas. It is also as succinct a statement of the philosophy undergirding Chesterton's own mysticism as you will find anywhere. As spirit in matter, we have an insatiable longing for pure beauty, pure being, and pure truth. Yet, here we are in this land of shadows and change and limitations. (For his epitaph Cardinal Newman chose *Ex Umbris in Veritatem: Out of the Shadows into the Truth.*) What we see is real being, only it is not, as Chesterton said, being all it could be.

Because of this tension between the "limited seen" and the "infinite unseen," we both underestimate and undervalue what we do see. We think, moreover, that we know more than we do about what we can't see. And what we can't see becomes more fascinating than what we can see. Of the all too many decadent scholastics, Chesterton said: "The world was cumbered with countless tomes, proving by logic a thousand things that can be known only to God." I think he would say the same about many "mere mystics." Here is his final statement:

> The deceitfulness of things which has had so sad an effect on so many sages, has almost a contrary effect on this sage [Thomas]. If things deceive us, it is by being more real than they seem. As ends in themselves they always deceive us; but as things tending to a greater end, they are even more real than we think them. If they seem to have a relative unreality (so to speak) it is because they are potential and not actual; they are unfulfilled, like packets of seeds or boxes of fireworks. They have it in them to be more real than they are. (18)

Because of his mystical intuition of the goodness of what he could see with his eyes, Chesterton was content to wait for the fireworks of eternity. Meanwhile, he did not want to miss this world in some kind of premature anticipation of the next. He knew that what he saw with his eyes was not all that he could reason to with his mind. But he found the actual goodness more captivating than an imagined or rational construct of the mind.

This is perfectly in keeping with his whole mysticism: penetration and insight into the present were more real for him than constructing an abstract theory about how the whole universe fits together and runs. His mysticism illuminates things as they are; he does not give us theories to help us abstract from what we can see, although he does acknowledge an ultimate manifestation of the structure of reality: "And there is an upper world of what the Schoolman called Fruition, or Fulfillment, in which all this relative relativity becomes actuality; in which the trees burst into flower or the rockets into flame" (180).

For Chesterton—at least in this present life—the light from without was more brilliant than the light within. He did not wish to go up into the sky in a balloon before his time. The highest branches of his tree did almost reach the stars anyhow. He would rather wait for the real flowers, see the actual explosions, than try to picture them in his mind.

> The mind conquers a new province like an emperor; but only because the mind has answered the bell like a servant. The mind has opened the doors and windows, because it is the natural activity of what is inside the house to find out what is outside the house. If the mind is sufficient to itself, it is insufficient for itself. For this feeding upon fact is itself; as an organ it has an object which is objective; this eating of the strange meat of reality. (184)

One of my favorite passages from Chesterton, and one which describes his own inner mind working on the stuff of creation, comes from *St. Thomas*. Chesterton is describing the saint's closing hours, and speaks of those standing around his bed. Again, I believe it is autobiographical: he is describing his own mind:

> They must have felt that, for that moment, the inside of the monastery was larger than the outside. It must have resembled the case of some mighty modern engine, shaking the ramshackle building in which it is for the moment enclosed. For truly that machine was made of the wheels of all the

worlds; and revolved like that cosmos of concentric spheres which, whatever its fate in the face of changing science, must always be something of a symbol for philosophy; the depth of double and triple transparencies more mysterious than darkness; the seven fold, the terrible crystal. In the world of that mind there was a wheel of angels, and a wheel of planets, and a wheel of plants or of animals; but there was also a just and intelligible order of all earthly things, a sane authority and a self-respecting liberty, and a hundred answers to a hundred questions in the complexity of ethics or economics. But there must have been a moment, when men knew that the thunderous mill of thought had stopped suddenly. (205)

Chesterton's mysticism included his own *"thunderous mill of thought."* The Immortally Active Presence was mediated to him through all the lovely things the Creator *was making at every moment.* The only mirror Chesterton didn't mind was the reflection of the truth of reality in his intellect, where, as Eternal Truth said to Catherine of Siena, he could gaze on the beauty of the Creator's creatures.

8

George MacDonald:
Chesterton's Inspiring Mystic

This is hardly a chapter, but as part of this brief study of Chesterton's mysticism I wanted to extend a tribute, as Chesterton does, to George MacDonald, the mystical man of letters of the nineteenth century. He was one Chesterton's inspirations.

In his introduction to *George MacDonald and His Wife* (1924), Grenville MacDonald's book about his parents, Chesterton pays supreme literary homage to a novel by MacDonald which, he says, changed his whole life. Often the question is posed to us: "What is the best book you have ever read?" Chesterton, for his part, says that this is not a realistic question to ask, since

> Our minds are mostly a vast uncatalogued library. But in a certain rather special sense I for one can really testify to a book that has made a difference to my whole existence, which helped me to see things in a certain way from the start; a vision of things which even so real a revolution as a change of religious allegiance has substantially only crowned and confirmed. Of all the stories I have read, including even all the novels of the same novelist, it remains the most real, the most realistic, in the exact sense of the phrase the most like life. It is called *The Princess and the Goblin,* and is by George MacDonald, the man who is the subject of this book.[1]

To put Chesterton's comments about MacDonald's influence

---

1 In *G. K. C. as M. C.*, J. P. de Fonseka (ed.), (London: Methuen & Co. Ltd., 1929), 163–164.

within a certain framework, it is worthwhile to turn to C. S. Lewis's introduction to MacDonald's fantasy novel *Lilith*, where he makes some very salient observations about the *kind of literature* Mac-Donald wrote. It is widely known that MacDonald was a fundamental inspiration for Lewis, who maintained that he never wrote a book without quoting him. He even went so far as to say that MacDonald's novel *Phantastes* converted and *baptized* his imagination at a time when Christianity was furthest from his mind:

> The whole book had about it a sort of cool, morning innocence, and also, quite unmistakably, a certain quality of death, *good* death. The quality which enchanted me in his imaginative works turned out to be the quality of the real universe, the divine, magical, terrifying and ecstatic reality in which we all live.[2]

What kind of literature did MacDonald write? From a literary point of view, Lewis rates it as third class. But in the kind of literature MacDonald wrote, the literary style is not the most important thing. MacDonald, Lewis points out, wrote

> fantasy that hovers between the allegorical and the mythopoetic. And this, in my opinion, he does better than any man. This art of myth-making does not essentially exist in *words* at all. In a myth—in a story where the mere pattern of events is all that matters—any means of communication whatever which succeeds in lodging those events in our imagination has, as we say, 'done the trick.' After that you can throw the means of communication away.[3]

In his *Autobiography,* Chesterton recalls how the truths of fairy tales endured as the foundational truths of his inner world. George MacDonald's *The Princess and the Goblins* was instrumental in preparing Chesterton's mind for Christian dogma. It would be a fascinating study, if it has not already been done, to draw parallels between the Christian truths in MacDonald's writings and Chesterton's own religious thinking.

---

2 "Introduction" to *Lilith* (Grand Rapids: Eerdmans, 1981), xi–xii.
3 Ibid., ix.

Chesterton describes for us the "home" truth, so to speak, with which his own imagination was baptized when he read *The Princess and the Goblins*. Through this book he was given an imaginative appreciation of the doctrine of original sin—which was fertile soil for the Holy Spirit to begin the process of his conversion:

When I say it is like life, what I mean is this. It describes a little princess living in a castle in the mountains which is perpetually undermined, so to speak, by subterranean demons who sometimes come up through the cellars. She climbs up the castle stairways to the nursery or the other rooms; but now and again the stairs do not lead to the usual landings, but to a new room she has never seen before, and cannot generally find again. Here a good great-grandmother, who is a sort of fairy godmother, is perpetually spinning and speaking words of understanding and encouragement. When I read it as a child, I felt that the whole thing was happening inside a real human house, not essentially unlike the house I was living in, which also had staircases and rooms and cellars. This is where the fairy-tale differed from many other fairy-tales; above all, this is where the philosophy differed from many other philosophies. I have always felt a certain insufficiency about the ideal of Progress, even of the best sort which is a Pilgrim's Progress. It hardly suggests how near both the best and the worst things are to us from the first; even perhaps especially at the first. I am speaking of what may emphatically be called the presence of household gods—and household goblins. And the picture of life in this parable is not only truer than the image of a journey like that of the Pilgrim's Progress, it is even truer than the mere image of a siege like that of the Holy War. There is something not only imaginative but intimately true about the idea of the goblins being below the house and capable of besieging it from the cellars. When the evil things besieging us do appear, they do not appear outside but inside.[4]

4 *G. K. C. as M. C.*, 164–165.

Chesterton had read in the Gospel the Lord's words about hatred, adultery, greed, murder, and so on, coming from within, from the heart, and that "nothing outside a man can defile him" (Mk. 7:20). This experience of the goblins coming from within is universal, only denied by people who will not take responsibility for their own actions. We do not "progress" away from the goblins; nor do we launch a final and successful attack upon the castle. To our dying day, we experience the goblins within and are called to an eternal vigilance.

What Lewis said of himself could be applied to Chesterton:

Now *Phantastes* was romantic enough in all conscience, but there was a difference. Nothing was at that time further from my thoughts than Christianity, and I therefore had no notion what this difference really was. I was only aware that if this new world was strange, it was also homely and humble, that if this was a dream, it was a dream in which one at least felt strangely vigilant.[5]

George MacDonald, through his Christian fantasies, buried deep within Chesterton's mind the seeds of truth. When Chesterton finally read the Gospels, the simple images of *The Princess* were "more corroborated than corrected when I came to give a more definite name to the lady watching over us from the turret, and perhaps to take a more practical view of the goblins under the floor."[6]

Throughout the course of writing this book I have been aware of MacDonald's gentle, mystical spirit. I believe, as Chesterton did, that he was a mystic. It is very probable that, if Chesterton has become one of our spiritual fathers of the 20th century, it is partially thanks to the spiritual fatherhood of George Mac-Donald. The Father from whom all fatherhood proceeds used MacDonald's wisdom to sow some of the first seeds of the Gospel in Chesterton's mind.

MacDonald was a man touched by the Spirit. While the actual mystical experience cannot be communicated to others, the

5 "Introduction" to *Lilith*, xi.
6 G. K. C. as M. C., 160.

insights derived from the mystic's primary contact with the Presence can be shared with others to their great spiritual profit. Often these insights re-emphasize some key truth about God or the deposit of faith that has fallen into abeyance on account of the temper of the times. In this way, MacDonald kindled others with the warmth of his mystical fire. God can raise up mystics like him in any place and at any time out of his tender mercy for his wayward children, to transcend the darkness of the times. I believe he has raised up Chesterton for this reason. The 20th century has surely been in need of genuine mystics.

Both Chesterton and Lewis point to the fact that MacDonald transcended his times. Lewis describes this uplifting action of the Holy Spirit in MacDonald's mysticism in terms of his escape from the Freudian formulas for dysfunction:

> We have learned from Freud and others about those distortions in character and errors in thought which result from a man's early conflicts with his father. Far the most important thing that we can know about George MacDonald is that his whole life illustrates the opposite process. An almost perfect relationship with his father was the earthly root of all his wisdom. From his own father, he said, he first learned that Fatherhood must be at the core of the universe. He was thus prepared in an unusual way to teach that religion in which the relation of Father and Son is of all relations the most central. He reports that he never, as boy or man, asked [his father] for anything without getting what he asked. Doubtless this tells us as much about the son's character as the father's. He who seeks the Father more than anything he can give, is likely to have what he asks, for he is not likely to ask amiss.[7]

It is common knowledge that Chesterton too was blessed with a deep and humanely good relationship with his own father. Joseph Pearce, in his biography of Chesterton, quotes E.C. Bentley, Chesterton's best friend, as saying that Chesterton "never met 'with greater kindliness—to say nothing of other sterling

---

7 "Introduction" to *Lilith*, iii–iv.

qualities—than that of his father, the businessman whose feeling for literature and all beautiful things worked so much upon his sons in childhood.'"[8]

Chesterton, drawing no doubt on his own balanced appreciation of fatherhood, commented on one of my own favorite sayings from MacDonald that I quoted above: "God is easy to please but hard to satisfy." He explains that some mystics who have not completed their tumbling try to satisfy God, and become too harsh, "just as some optimists are doubtless too much occupied with insisting that He is easy to please."

MacDonald could easily have become a forerunner of the New Age movement, like Blake; or a precursor of the complete reduction of the Christian faith to anthropology, like Feuerbach; or a prototype of the denial of God and the reduction of all inner life to the psyche, like Freud. But he became, as Chesterton asserts, a "morning star" of the reunion of Christendom:

> MacDonald made for himself a sort of spiritual environment, a space and transparency of mystical light, which was quite exceptional in his national and denominational environment. He said things that were like the Cavalier mystics, like the Catholic saints, sometimes perhaps like the Platonists or the Swedenborgians, but not in the least like the Calvinists. And when he comes to be more carefully studied as a mystic, as I think he will be when people discover the possibility of collecting jewels scattered in a rather irregular setting, it will be found, I fancy, that he stands for a rather important turning-point in the history of Christendom. As Protestants speak of the morning stars of the Reformation, we may be allowed to note such names here and there as morning stars of the Reunion.[9]

Chesterton, too, I believe, was a mystic, a bright morning star of authentic Catholic mysticism in the 20th century. Not only is his teaching a guide to orthodox faith, but his *mysticism* is a light

---

8 *Wisdom and Innocence: A Life of G.K. Chesterton* (London: Hodder & Stoughton Ltd, 1996), 4.

9 G.K. Chesterton, *William Blake* (New York: Duckworth & Co., 1910), 168.

guiding our path through the dark forest. And perhaps the greatest blackness in that forest has been the erroneous belief, born of fear, that to love the good things of the earth is an obstacle to God and Christ, and that we must choose between the two realities.

Not so! Rightly understood, these created realities are the very place where the Good God can be especially experienced. Chesterton had a vivid, uncommon appreciation of the Presence in the good things he could see with his eyes: "I do not think there is anyone who takes quite such fierce pleasure in things being themselves as I do."[10]

In his "Prayer in Darkness," in which he frames this "fierce pleasure" of his in the poignant language of poetry, Chesterton caps his thoughts, in the last stanza, with an extraordinary allusion to Christ on Calvary:

> This much, O heaven—if I should brood or rave,
> Pity me not; but let the world be fed,
> Yea, in my madness, if I strike me dead,
> Heed you the grass that grows upon my grave.
> If I dare snarl between this sun and sod,
> Whimper and clamour, give me grace to own,
> In sun and rain and fruit in season shown,
> The shining silence of the scorn of God.
> Thank God the stars are set beyond my power,
> If I must travail in a night of wrath,
> Thank God my tears will never vex a moth,
> Nor any curse of mine cut down a flower.
> Men say the sun was darkened: yet I had
> Thought it beat brightly, even on—Calvary:
> And He that hung upon the Torturing Tree
> Heard all the crickets singing, and was glad.[11]

---

10 Ibid., 168–169.
11 *The Works of G.K. Chesterton* (Hertfordshire: Wordsworth Editions, 1995), 117.

PART III

SOME MYSTICS WHO LANDED ON THEIR HEADS

9

William Blake:
A Tragic Mystic

For enthusiastic Chestertonians like myself one of the most deli-
cious pleasures in life is to come across a work of the great man
that you have not read before. There are still quite a number of
these for the present author, but receiving a copy of *William
Blake*[1] was particularly exhilarating, seeing as I was engaged in
this study of Chesterton's mysticism. My desire to read this book
was first whetted when I came across an unsigned review of it in
Conlon's *The Critical Judgments*. The reviewer claims that:

> Blake's commerce with the other world is called 'spiritual-
> ism,' which is about as far from a comprehension of the
> truth as anything could be. But it is really Blake the mystic
> that Mr. Chesterton most completely fails to appreciate, and
> this in spite of a lot of excellent talk about mysticism in gen-
> eral. Mr. Chesterton is quite pleased that Blake should have
> been a mystic, for that gives him something to hit the agnos-
> tics with; but he has no notion of a mysticism, which
> requires some pretty close investigation to discover its
> meaning. And when he calls Blake mad, using the same
> 'incomprehensible' phrase in several places, he is making
> out Jallaludin-Rumi and every other eastern mystic mad as
> well.[2]

1 G.K. Chesterton, *William Blake* (New York: Duckworth & Co., 1910).
Page references in this section refer to this book unless otherwise noted.
2 D.J. Conlon (ed.), *The Critical* Judgments, Part I (Antwerp: University
Faculty of St. Ignatius, 1976), 256–58.

True enough, Chesterton does indeed see a sort of madness in eastern mysticism. But the phrase which initially caught my eye was the reference to "a lot of excellent talk about mysticism." And when he says that Chesterton "has no notion of a mysticism," well, I thought to myself, "I just have to get my hands on that book."

As I was coming to the end of my study without having yet obtained the book, I was bemoaning the fact that I probably would not be able to situate its approach to mysticism within the chronology of Chesterton's development as I had been trying to do with his other ideas on the subject. When, however, I finally received the book, I was able to see that it put the capstone on my research and provided me with an excellent framework for a conclusion that complemented my findings; and it is not out of place as a middle chapter in this study of Chesterton's mysticism.

In *William Blake*, which came out in 1910, I found almost all of the ideas about mysticism that he would develop in his subsequent writings. I don't know if our disgruntled reviewer lived to read *St. Francis of Assisi* and *St. Thomas Aquinas*, but he would have found there the "pretty close investigation" of mysticism that he did not find in *William Blake*. He did not find it, because Chesterton was just beginning to develop his ideas. But the seeds are all there, as they often are in the youthful work of men of genius.

"Was Blake mad?" Probably many people who have studied Blake in school (as I have not) have had some such question posed to them in a test, or maybe they even wrote a paper on it. Having seen references to this query often enough, I was tempted to answer it, like Chesterton, with a qualified affirmative and entitle this section "Blake: the Mad Mystic." However, after completing the book, I experienced a keen sense of sadness about Blake, akin to the sadness I felt about historical figures like Savonarola and the Fraticelli who, as we shall see, did not land back on their feet in the real world after all their tumultuous, eccentric tumblings.

In our culture, "mad" means "insane," "out of one's mind," "having hallucinations," "not all there," or, as is sometimes expressed here locally in the wilds of Canada, "having only one oar in the water." According to Chesterton, Blake was not mad in this sense. He does not call him tragic, but that's the word that seems to fit his life and work. Webster says that in tragedy "the leading character is by some passion and limitation brought to a catastrophe, and this excites pity and terror." In my opinion, this definition fits Blake perfectly.

To "pity" I would add "sadness," sadness that he did not discover, like Chesterton, the Catholic faith to help him understand and control his mysticism. "Terror" may seem like a strong word, but we should indeed be terrified at what can happen to people who are catapulted into the supernatural world without the guidance of the Church.

Our dissatisfied critic objected to calling Blake's experiences of the supernatural world (or, as Chesterton sometimes calls it, the unnatural world) "spiritualism." We shall see, however, that, in his study, Chesterton gives a very profound description of spiritualism, situating it in its historical context. In any case, I hope our critic is now himself in the true land of the supernatural with Christ and the angels, enjoying the opportunity to discuss his criticisms with the key disputants, Chesterton and Blake.

Blake as Mystic

It was Chesterton's opinion that Blake was a mystic: "Like so many other starry philosophers and flaming mystics, he came out of a shop" (3). This seems to be an obvious allusion to St. Francis, whose father, with his textile business, was one of the rising bourgeois, one of the first of those who, as Christopher Dawson remarked, "made money," a totally new phenomenon in the Christian world. He asserts that "Blake saw the oddest people in his visions, people with whom neither he nor anyone else has anything particular to do. That is one of the facts that makes one fancy that Blake's visions were genuine" (14–15). Further on Chesterton states, in rather grand terms, that "like every great mystic, he was also a great rationalist" (83).

An early principle of Chesterton about mysticism in this comment about Blake is that, in a limited sense of the word, one can be a mystic, that is, have powerful experiences of the supernatural world, without being either orthodox, or holy, or completely sane. The experiences can be authentic, but one can misinterpret them; or they can come from sources other than the Lord; or one can lack the "other oar in the water" to avoid going around in circles.

There is a story from Blake's early childhood describing an occasion when

> he lingered too long in the fields and came back to tell his mother that he had seen the prophet Ezekiel sitting under a tree. His mother smacked him. Thus ended the first adventure of William Blake in that wonderland of which he was a citizen. (4)

There is nothing in Chesterton's book which implies that he did not believe that Blake probably really did see Ezekiel. He even goes so far as to consider him a citizen of that wonderland, by which he means the world of the supernatural in a non-pejorative sense.

On another occasion, still as a child, Blake saw a tree filled with angels, which he depicts in one of his drawings. The Encyclopedia Britannica (Vol. 2) explains these visions by saying that Blake had a rare psychological capacity, the eidic sense, whereby the images in the imagination take on a solidity as if seen outside the mind. Maybe so. But this still does not explain Blake's seeing things he did not know about or was not capable of imagining. What, for instance, does a little boy know about the prophet Ezekiel?

Although we will find in Chesterton's *William Blake* some deep insights into the true nature of mysticism, Chesterton's mature reflections are found, as we saw, in *St. Francis* and *St. Thomas*. In *William Blake*, rather, we find an in-depth treatment of what makes mystics go off-base, especially mystics of the modern world who are without the guidance of the Church. For this reason, being rudderless, they lack some of the fundamental virtues of the genuine mystic. Blake is an outstanding example of the mystic soul trying to grow up in a period of rationalism and decadent Christianity.

At the end of the book Chesterton said that

William Blake: A Tragic Mystic

William Blake was frequently reproached for his tenderness towards Catholicism; but it would have surprised him very much to be told that he would join it. But he would have joined it—if he had lived a thousand years, or even perhaps a hundred. (208–09)

Unfortunately, Blake only lived 70 years (1757–1827). And what if he had lived in the ages of faith? Yeats makes the following acutely perceptive observation:

He was a man crying out for a mythology, and trying to make one because he could not find one to his hand. Had he been born a Catholic of Dante's time he would have been well content with Mary and the angels.[3]

The rationalistic and highly Protestant age in which he actually lived did not offer him much help to understand his visions. Chesterton says, at the very outset of his book, that "anybody's biography ought to begin with the words, 'In the beginning God created heaven and earth.' For the sake of brevity, however, all books have to be begun in the wrong way" (1–2). So Chesterton, too, starts in the wrong way, considering the spiritual atmosphere of the 18th century. The abbreviated account of the tragedy of William Blake, the mystic, begins with the historical period in which he was born. The "Three Strands" can be a guide for evaluating any mystic of any age.

The Three Strands

Every man of us today is three men. There is in every modern European three powers so distinct as to be almost personal, 'the trinity of our earthly destiny.' They are the Christian, the man of the historic Church, of the creed; the Roman that makes straight roads and clear laws, and for whom good sense is good enough. The third man—he is

---

3 W.B. Yeats, "Blake's Illustrations to Dante," *Essays and Introductions* (London: Macmillan 1961), 114.

harder to speak of. He is the origins—he is the man of the forest. (106–07)

The pagan gods were dead long before Christianity. They were replaced by the deified Emperor, who was called "Divus Caesar":

> In one sense, because Christianity revived belief in the spiritual world, there was a "kind of clamorous resurrection of all the old supernatural instincts of the forest and the hill. But it put upon this occult chaos the Roman idea of balance and sanity. In short, Christianity (merely historically seen) can best be understood as an attempt to combine the reason of the market-place with the mysticism of the forest. It was an attempt to accept all the superstitions that are necessary to man and to be philosophical at the end of them. Pagan Rome has sought to bring order or reason among men. Christian Rome sought to bring order and reason among the gods. (108)

Much has been written about the rise of the so-called Enlightenment in the 18th century. If any "virile mind" of that century expressed anything that could not be rationally explained, they were labeled "enthusiast as a term of scorn. All that we call mysticism they called madness" (112–13).

These three men, of which Chesterton says each one of us is comprised, are not like strata of a rock, but the strands of a rope. Since they have come into existence, no one strand of the three can be unraveled from the rope without the other two also being untwined and becoming limp and weak. The first unraveling of the Christian strand in the 18th century resulted in humanitarianism, or compassion for the individual. "This personal humanitarianism is the relic of Christianity—perhaps (if I may say so) the dregs of Christianity. Of this humanitarianism or sentimentalism, or whatever it can best be called, Blake was the enthusiastic inheritor" (117). "This irrational individual pity is the purely Christian element in the eighteenth century. This irrational individual pity is the purely Christian element in William Blake" (118).

At the same time, in the 18th century, the Roman strand of reason and order was being detached from the Church and reshaped into a grotesque parody of enlightenment. This left the "man of the forest," who was also set loose and unraveled, as it were, from his companions, the Christian and the Roman. The occult residues of this element, which consisted of paganism and pagan magic, were never completely absent or eradicated by the tempering forces of Christianity. Now they were going to resurge with a vengeance. "Christianity, rightly or wrongly, always discouraged it on the grounds that it was, or tended to be, black magic" (120). In all my reading about the Enlightenment I have not come across such an incisive treatment of this other aspect of the age—the release of the old gods—so important for understanding the spiritualism which accompanied that age:

> Now the eighteenth century was primarily the release (as its leaders held) of reason from the control of the Church. But when the Church was once really weakened, it was the release of many other things. It was not the release of reason only, but of a more ancient unreason. It was not the release of the natural, but also of the supernatural, and also, alas! of the unnatural. The heathen mystics hidden for two thousand years came out of their caverns. Of this particular kind of supernaturalism, Blake is particularly the heir. Mysticism marks an effort to escape from or even to forget the historic Christian, and especially the Catholic Church. (123–24)

This era marks the waxing strength of secret theosophical societies, such as the Masons. Blake did not belong to these societies, "for, to tell the truth, he had some difficulty in belonging to any society," but he did develop his own secret language much of which, to this day, scholars admit remains quite undecipherable. Blake was deficient in his education. Also, he stood at the beginning of a new era. Without Catholicism to guide the "forest man" in him, he "really had to begin at the beginning, because it was a different beginning" (126).

The Mystic Who Makes Mysteries

Beginning, then, at the beginning, Blake trusted and followed no tradition. He proceeded, therefore, to make up his own unseen world—a true gnostic. This led him to obscurity and mystification. He often used words with meanings known only to himself. This fact of Blake's mysteriousness, in the negative sense, which all the commentators agree upon, prompted Chesterton to elaborate one of the fundamental trademarks of true mysticism: *it illuminates, it does not obscure.* As he explains:

> A verbal accident has confused the mystical with the mysterious. Mysticism is generally felt vaguely to be itself vague—a thing of clouds and curtains, of darkness or concealing vapours, of bewildering conspiracies or impenetrable symbols. Some quacks have indeed dealt in such things: but no true mystic ever loved darkness rather than light. No pure mystic ever loved mere mystery. The mystic does not bring doubts or riddles: the doubts and riddles exist already.
>
> The mystic is not the man who makes mysteries but the man who destroys them. The mystic may be true or false, but which is always comprehensible—by which I mean, not that it is always comprehended, but it always can be comprehended, because there is always something to comprehend. The man whose meaning remains mysterious fails, I think, as a mystic: and Blake did often fail in this way. (131–32)

When you read the works of genuine mystics such as St. Catherine of Siena, St. Teresa of Avila, St. John of the Cross, St. Augustine, and St. Gregory of Nyssa, you are struck by this quality of luminous clarity. Reading them is like having your mind washed with truth as in a warm bath. Some passages are very deep and profound and may require several readings. But this lack of comprehension is due to one's own ignorance or lack of spiritual insight, not the intractability of the material. "Profound" does not mean "obscure" or "incomprehensible." This is what Chesterton means by "there is always something to be comprehended." As you grow in your own spiritual life, or if you spend some time studying the background of certain passages, reading commentators, and so on, you can come to an understanding of these works. They are ultimately *understandable.*

On the other hand, the Church sometimes issues a caution, a *monitum,* concerning the writings of certain authors precisely because She herself doesn't quite know what they mean, has not been able to understand them, and is afraid they may lead to error. Mysticism, understood as a powerful experience of the supernatural world, does not guarantee clarity or orthodoxy.

Evidently a certain clergyman, a Rev. Dr. Trusler, had difficulties with Blake's ideas. Blake wrote to him: "You say that I want somebody to Elucidate my Ideas. But you ought to know that What is Grand is necessarily obscure to Weak men. That which can be made Explicit to the Idiot is not worth my care. The wisest of the Ancients consider'd what is not too Explicit as the fittest for Instruction, because it rouzes the faculties to act. I name Moses, Solomon, Esop, Homer, Plato."[4] This stands as a perfect illustration of what Chesterton means when he says that the false mystic is one who loves mysteries.

Powerful experiences, precisely because they are powerful, carry along with them a conviction of their authenticity. But the sincerity of the recipient is no guarantee of the truthfulness of the experiences. One can be sincerely mistaken and deluded. Blake always expressed himself with great assurance and certainty: "We always feel that he is saying something very plain and emphatic, even when we have not the wildest notion of what it is" (132).

It is not necessary, for the purposes of this book, to consider the spiritual and mental distortions which flowed from Blake's false gnostic world. I will simply review Chesterton's conclusions about him. At the end of *William Blake* he tried to sort out the wheat from the chaff.

When Chesterton is contrasting Buddhism and Christianity, the differences are quite clear and very marked. Blake is another matter altogether. All throughout the poet's mythological world are these "dregs of Christianity," which means that Chesterton has to do some very fine discerning, in order to bring to light his (Chesterton's) own understanding of true Christian mysticism. In the following passage, perhaps none of these positive elements in Blake's vision are unmixed with tares. Yet even so, Chesterton does see him as not succumbing to Tibet. He is a truly tragic fig-

---

4 Extract from the Letter from William Blake to Dr. Trusler, 23 August 1799.

ure in having been exposed to a rather decadent Christianity and in having tried to salvage what he thought was authentic. His salvage operation was not successful. Here's how Chesterton tried to sort it out at the end of his study:

> He was on the side of historic Christianity on the fundamental question on which it confronts the East; the idea that personality is the glory of the universe and not its shame; that creation is higher than evolution, because it is more personal; that pardon is higher than Nemesis, because it is more personal; that the forgiveness of sins is essential to the communion of saints; and the resurrection of the body to the life everlasting.
>
> Against all emasculate mysticism Blake, like a Titan, rears his colossal figure and his earthquake voice. Through all the cloud and chaos of his stubborn symbolism and his perverse theories, through the tempest of exaggeration and the full midnight of madness, he reiterates with passionate precision that only that which is lovable can be adorable, that deity is either a person or a puff of wind, that the more we know of higher things the more palpable and incarnate we shall find them; that the form filling the heavens is the likeness of the appearance of a man. (209–10)

The first great lesson we might draw from these remarks for any would-be mystic is this: don't be a mystic on your own. A mark of the true mystic, as noted above, is an absolute orthodoxy. The genuine mystic is deeply imbedded in—*and trusts*—the tradition in which he lives and moves and has his being. Blake had no tradition, trusted no Church, was a loner in his thinking, and sought to map out the unseen world completely on his own.

"Was Blake Mad?"

We have now established that, in Chesterton's view, Blake, even though he was not an orthodox Christian, was a mystic and that the larger, historical causes of his bizarre mythology can be traced to his having been born in an age of weakened Christianity, which witnessed the rise of science and a new paganism.

What, though, were some of the more personal spiritual and psychological causes of Blake's distorted mythology? As far as I know, *William Blake* is Chesterton's most sustained commentary on the world of false mystics. It contains, therefore, errors which Chesterton himself was aware of and avoided. This brings us to a consideration of Blake's mental condition.

Blake was not mad in the sense that he was unable to function practically. He was a citizen, managed property, and was generally quite business-like. Nor was he mad in the sense of being a depressed person and melancholic: "He was in contact with all the songs and smells of the universe, and he was entirely guiltless of that one evil element which is almost universal in the character of the morbidly insane—I mean secrecy" (71–72).

Nor was he mad in the sense that he was unreasonable or inconsistent in his thinking: "Blake was one of the most consistent men that ever lived, both in theory and practice. Blake may have been quite wrong, but he was not in the least unreasonable" (72). Nor can he be called mad because he claimed to have visions, except by dogmatic sceptics who deny the reality or possibility of visions.

What was it, then, that lay at the root of Blake's mental condition? If I understand Chesterton correctly, he would say that if Blake had taken a modern psychological test, the experts would not have found that his mental faculties were impaired. But if the question, "Do you ever have visions?" had been posed to Blake by these same modern psychologists, he would have answered, "but of course." In that case, they would have labeled him as mentally unbalanced, relying, as mentioned above, on the dogmatic scepticism of their profession, which holds that "sane men do not have visions."

Chesterton, for his part, while eschewing the skepticism of the psychologists, attributes Blake's mental imbalance to the spiritual disorder inherent in his visions rather than the visions as such. He claims that it was precisely the nature of his visions which was the cause of something in Blake's reason that "had been broken (or cracked) by something but what there was of it was reasonable" (83). Here are Chesterton's conclusions about Blake's madness:

I firmly believe that what did hurt Blake's brain was the reality of his spiritual communications. It will generally be found, I think, with some important exceptions, that whenever Blake talked most about inspiration, he was actually least inspired. That is, he was least inspired by whatever spirit presides over good poetry and good thinking. He was abundantly inspired by whatever spirit presides over bad poetry or bad thinking. Whatever god specialises in unreadable and almost unpronounceable verse was certainly present when he invented the extraordinary history of 'William Bond,' or the maddening metre of the lines 'To Mr. Butts.' Whatever archangel rules over utter intellectual error had certainly spread his wings of darkness over Blake when he came to the conclusion that a man ought to be bad in order to be pardoned. I really believe that this was not from Blake, but from his spirits. It is all very well for great men, like Mr. Reset and Mr. Swinburne, to trust utterly to the seraphim of Blake. They may naturally trust angels— they do not believe in them. But I do believe in angels, and incidentally in fallen angels. (96–97)

Could Chesterton say any more clearly that he thought Blake's visions were either inspired or distorted by evil spirits? Blake's *certainty* came from the reality of his visions, whereas his preposterous mythology came from their content and/or his interpretation of them. Catholicism entered the world to bring order into the gods. Without that order, visions are dangerous. There is no such thing as neutrality in the supernatural world. It is not just a morally indifferent matrix. Spirits, good and evil, inhabit it. Evil spirits were mixed up with Blake's visions. That is Chesterton's conclusion.

The critic quoted at the beginning (96) objected to Chesterton reducing Blake's vision to "spiritualism," but that is exactly what it is, as Chesterton argues. He goes on to describe the difference between the genuine mystical world of the Christian and the world of spiritualism:

There is no danger to health in being a mystic: but there may be some danger to health in being a spiritualist. It would be a very poor pun to say that a taste for spirits is bad for the health; nevertheless, oddly enough, though a poor pun, it is a perfectly correct philosophical parallel. The difference between having a real religion and having a mere curiosity about religion and having a mere curiosity about psychic marvels is really very like the difference between drinking beer and drinking brandy, between drinking wine and drinking gin. Beer is a food as well as a stimulant; so a positive religion is a comfort as well as an adventure. A man drinks his wine because it is his favorite wine, the pleasure of his palate or the vintage of his valley. A man drinks alcohol merely because it is alcohol. So a man calls upon his gods because they are good or at any rate good to him, because they are the idols that protect his tribe or the saints that have blessed his birthday. But spiritualists call upon spirits merely because they are spirits; they ask for ghosts merely because they are ghosts.

A taste for spiritualism is very like a taste for spirits. The man who drinks gin or methylated spirit does it only because it makes him super-normal; so the man who with tables or planchettes invokes supernatural beings invokes them only because they are supernatural. He does not know that they are good or wise or helpful. He knows he desires the deity, but he does not even know that he likes him. He attempts to invoke the god without adoring him. He is interested in whatever he can find out touching supernatural existence; but he is not really filled with joy as by the face of a divine friend, any more than anyone actually likes the taste of methylated spirit. In such psychic investigations, in a word, there is excitement, but not affectional satisfaction; there is brandy but no food. (98–100)

Pace our reviewer who disagreed that Blake was a spiritualist, Chesterton gives here some profound discernment between a spiritualist and a genuine mystic. First of all, genuine mystics do not seek spiritual experiences or visions. Our whole tradition is against it. But if they do find themselves being gifted with such visions, their attitude is altogether different from those who seek such experiences in ignorance, or out of curiosity, or without being sure with whom exactly they will be in communication.

Spiritualism is still among us, and the New Age movement is simply a modern term for it. Modern people are hungering for something more than the material world; they are seeking the super-natural or, we might say, the unnatural world. They do so without knowing whom they will meet in this world. They may be loving people, but being ignorant of the gods they may contact, how can they love them? And their biggest and most dangerous error is the mere fact that they are seeking, by some technique, to get into this unnatural world. Their efforts are similar to the spiritualist parlor games of the early part of the century. Chesterton knew all about them: he participated in some.

Curiosity of this kind is certainly fraught with danger. It is Chesterton's opinion that Blake, even granted the reality of his visions, was a spiritualist in the sense described above. His visions were intoxicating, and he did not know to whom he was speaking or whom he was watching. He said naively to a friend, Crabb Robinson, "Dante saw devils where I saw none. I see good only."[5] Evidently, therefore, he was under the illusion that he saw only good angels in his visions, an assertion that Chesterton disputes:

> Now Blake was in the most reckless, and sometimes even in the most vulgar, sense a spiritualist. He threw the doors of his mind open to what the late George MacDonald called in a fine phrase 'the canaille of the other world.' I think it is impossible to look at some of the pictures which Blake drew, under what he considered direct spiritual dictation, without feeling that he was from time to time under influences that were not only evil but even foolishly evil. (100)

"Canaille" was a new word for me. Webster defines it thus: "(F., fr., It. *canaglia*, orig. a pack of dogs, fr. L. *canis*, dog.) The lowest class of people; the rabble; the riffraff." When people try to enter the supernatural world out of curiosity, or without knowing what god they will encounter, they encounter not the hounds of Heaven, but a pack of wild dogs, the dregs, the riffraff

5 Yeats, ibid., 131.

of the world of spiritual beings. In this way, these sinister spirits are literally given an opening to sport with us and tease us with their shifting demeanor. They can be openly malevolent, or else put on a good show as angels of light, or even be impishly foolish. Without the guidance of the Church or of an experienced spiritual director, people become the playthings of these spirits.

Chesterton mentions a bizarre drawing that Blake made, claiming that it came in a vision. The drawing, which Blake called *The Man Who Built the Pyramids*, is described by Chesterton as portraying:

> The face of an idiot. Nay, we behold even the face of an evil idiot, a leering, half-witted face with no chin and the protuberant nose of a pig. Blake declared that he drew this face from a real spirit, and I see no reason to doubt that he did. [But] that vision of swinish silliness was really a bad vision to have, it left a smell of demoniac silliness behind it. (101)

An orthodox Christian knows and loves the Lord without seeing him. Should he be granted a vision, he will recognize him whom he has not seen. Also, he will recognize if it is not the Lord, because he knows by faith, the face of his Lord.

Also, *humility* is the great protector of the mystic. There is a relevant story from one of the desert fathers who had a vision of an angel, who said to him: "The Lord has sent me to you." The humble little father answered: "I don't know any reason why the Lord would visit me." And the devil left him.

And, paradoxically, a genuine love for God will also be a protection to our spirit, if we are granted a vision of him: "The tragedy of the spiritualist simply is that he has to know his gods before he loves them. But a man ought to love his gods before he is sure that there are any. The sublime words of St. John's Gospel permit of a sympathetic parody; if a man love not God whom he has not seen, how shall he love God whom he has seen?" (102).

Blake, the lonely sceptic, did not believe in the gods until he saw them. But what gods did he see, not having any tradition to help him know and discern? Like the New Agers who were to follow in his wake, he simply opened his mind to whoever was there, as Chesterton points out:

But a mystic like Blake simply puts up a placard for the whole universe, like an old woman letting lodgings. The mansion of his mind was indeed a magnificent one; but no one must be surprised if the first man that walked into it was 'the man who built the pyramids.' (102)

Blake as a Faddist

It has been noted that the necessity for the mind to have fixed points of truth is one of Chesterton's great themes. It is here that Blake fails egregiously. Certainly the Catholic Church would see him as unorthodox and heretical. In this context of the false mysticism of Blake, Chesterton develops the splendid notion of heresy as a fad, arguing that

> In either case the definition of the fad or heresy is not so very difficult. A fad or heresy is the exaltation of something which, even if true, is secondary or temporary in its nature against those things which are essential and eternal, those things which always prove themselves true in the long run. In short, it is the setting up of the mood against the mind. (167–68)

(He says somewhere else that Rome is waiting for the end of all fads.) Chesterton then enumerates a number of things, some of which would not be in the category of a doctrine of the faith, but nonetheless are among those aberrations which ascetics and mystics are prone to raise to the status of a dogma. As has already been noted, Chesterton is not against the wild asceticism of the desert, nor is he opposed to the Simons of the spiritual Olympics sitting on top of pillars to their hearts' content. Rather he is on guard lest their asceticism and mysticism so overwhelm their minds that their powerful experiences are trumpeted to the world as the way everyone should go. They risk mistaking their personal inspirations for the eternal truths that everyone else should embrace.

The War of the Mystics

Chesterton was a fighter, engaged in battle. What was he fighting for? Many things: truth in Christian doctrine; the rights of the common man; a poetic and adventuresome approach to life; the restoration of wonder. But in the context of this tentative exploration of his mysticism, I came across a pronouncement which gives yet another target to his marching orders.

It is a pronouncement that arises out of his consideration, in due course, of what was positive in Blake's vision of reality. As he makes clear:

> When we have fairly stated this doubtful and even false element in Blake's philosophy, we can go on with greater ease and thoroughness to state where the solid and genuine value of that philosophy lay. (183)

He does, however, preface his treatment of Blake's genuine value with this remark about false mystics, situating them in a broader frame of reference within the history of ideas:

> It is not unnatural that they should have fallen into many errors, employed dangerous fallacies, and even ruined the earth for the sake of the cloudland. But the war in which they were engaged has been none the less the noblest and most important effort of human history, and in their whole army there was no greater warrior than Blake. (183)

Chesterton goes on to say that the fundamental question involved in mysticism "is so enormous and so important, that it is difficult to state even by reason of its reality" (196). He makes ready to treat, at a very profound level, a question he considers, in some way, fundamental to all else. In this final discussion, Blake, generally speaking, comes out on the right side, so long as we keep his fads and heresies in view.

People who really understand the human condition consider true mystics as having the final word about reality. They are the elite of the human race, those who have come in communion with the Presence. This is why some thinkers look to the mystics as having the ultimate vision.

The point here is that the mystics are engaged in a war that is extremely "noble and important"; indeed, Chesterton states that it is "the most important." Mystics are considered the full flowering of the human race, people who have entered the bright darkness and the cloud of unknowing and returned to tell us of the nature of reality. The war in which they are engaged is of the highest importance and relevance.

Their field of action is described in martial terms as a war, precisely because different visions of God and reality are competing for the great palm of ultimate truth. It is quite a prize to have the last word about human existence. In this battle of the mystics, "there are two types of mysticism, that of Christendom and that of Orientalism" (201). In this battle, moreover, Blake is on the right side. We start out in life being aware of details; then the mind seeks to discover the grand design of reality, as Chesterton explains, using his martial metaphor:

> It is the design that we only see very slowly; and some men die never having seen it at all. We all wake up on a battlefield. Wait until you know what the battle is broadly about before you rush roaring after any advancing regiment. For a battle is a complicated thing; each army contains coats of different colour; each section of each army advances at a different angle. (197–98)

It is at this point that we encounter some of Chesterton's most profound reflections on the challenges of the human condition. He proceeds now to tell us what the main mystical battle is all about, after declaring that Blake, in some essential areas, wears the colors of Christendom: "There is an everlasting battle in which Blake is on the side of the angels, and what is much more difficult and dangerous, on the side of all the sensible men" (196).

The Solidity of God

It is helpful, in approaching this key stage of Chesterton's argument, to call to mind his definition of a mystic: someone who believes that two worlds are better than one. Since this is so, both the world we see and the world we cannot see are real and clear, with definite designs, as well as luminous. The true mystic, moreover, does not conceal mysteries, but rather *reveals* them. Nor does the true mystic communicate things no one else can understand. What is more, he does not deny one world in favor of the other. Basically, Chesterton sets out to say that Blake was essentially right about the *reality and solidity* of the unseen world (though he has false interpretations of it), but that he was less than clear and enthusiastic about the world that he could see. In other words, he was a mystic with his feet in only one world.

In addition, Blake had these essential elements of a true mystic: brightness of colour and clearness of shape. His drawings are clear, even if their significance is doubtful.

> But in the work of a real mystic the triangle is a hard mathematical triangle not to be mistaken for a cone or a polygon. The Christian decorators, being true mystics, were chiefly concerned to maintain the reality of objects. For the highest dogma of the spiritual is to affirm the material. This decision of tint and outline belongs not only to Blake's pictures, but even to his poetry. Even in his descriptions there is no darkness, and practically, in the modern sense, no distance. All his animals are as absolute as the animals on a shield of heraldry. (135–36)

This leads Chesterton into a discussion about realism, in which he points out where Blake is in agreement with the platonic and scholastic tradition. Modern realists begin at the outside of things; medieval realists began at the inside. They were keenly concerned with the original idea of things, the *quidditas*, the thingness of a thing, as they would say, delving into the essences of things, of elephants, for instance. Blake mirrored them with a similar interest in thingness and essences:

> When you have quite realised this ancient sense in the reality of an elephant, go back and read William Blake's poems about animals, as, for instance, about the lamb and about the tiger. You will see quite clearly that he is talking of an eternal tiger, who rages and rejoices forever in the sight of God. You will see that he is talking of an eternal and super-

natural lamb, who can only feed happily in the fields of heaven. (137)

Remember that Chesterton as a young man had a skirmish with impressionism in art, and how it nearly drove him mad. He was led to doubt whether the world outside of him really existed; he was tempted to suppose it existed only in his mind. He returns to those memories here, using them as a springboard for his discussion of Blake.

> Impressionism is a form of scepticism, inasmuch as it tends to the belief that one's impressions of reality are more real than the essence that one cannot see. It means believing one's immediate impressions at the expense of one's more permanent and positive generalisations. It puts what one notices above what one knows. It means the monstrous heresy that seeing is believing. (137–38)

The following passages are essential to Chesterton's understanding of Blake as an anti-Impressionist realist: "On this point he is at one with all the mystics and with all the saints" (141). Blake is not drawing mere symbols or allegories. When Blake made the lamb the symbol of innocence,

> he meant that there really is behind the universe an eternal image called the Lamb, of which all living lambs are merely the copies or the approximations. He held that eternal innocence to be an actual and even an awful thing. It is merely that Blake did not mean that meekness was true and the lamb only a pretty fable. If anything he meant that meekness was a mere shadow of the everlasting lamb. The distinction is essential to anyone at all concerned for this rooted spirituality which is the only enduring sanity of mankind. The personal is not a mere figure for the impersonal; rather the impersonal is a clumsy term for something more personal than common personality. God is not a symbol of goodness. Goodness is a symbol of God. (141–42)

The Impressionists, for their part, believe that the appearances are more real than the essence:

A white cow at one particular instant of the evening light may be gold on one side and violet on the other. The whole point of Impressionism is to say that there is no white cow at all. But the essence of mysticism is to insist that there is a white cow, however veiled with shadow or painted with sunset gold. Blessed are they who have seen the violet cow and who yet believe in the white cow. To the mystic a white cow had a sort of solid whiteness, as if the cow were made out of frozen milk. (138)

Chesterton now applies this understanding of realism to Blake's concept of God. To illustrate his point, he first quotes these lines from "The Auguries of Innocence": "God appears and God is light, to those poor souls that dwell in night. But does a human form display to those that dwell in realms of clay." In reading the following explication of these lines by Chesterton, keep in mind his revulsion at the Eastern impersonal All, to which he gave the pejorative epithet, Tibet:

But those last two lines express all that is best in Blake and all that is best in all the tradition of the mystics. This is the point about Blake that must be understood if nothing else is understood. God for him was not more and more vague and diaphanous as one came near to Him. God was more and more solid as one came near. When one was far off one might fancy Him to be impersonal. When one came into personal relation one knew that He was a person. The personal God was a fact. The impersonal God of the Pantheists was a kind of condescending symbol. (147–48)

Blake's idea of God is certainly not orthodox. He does not believe in a Pure Spirit penetrating creation, but distinct from it. Nonetheless, he is on the side of the angels in that his God is personal, and he can relate to him as a person. Thus he is to be numbered among those who champion "the idea that personality is the glory of the universe and not its shame" (209). Accordingly, "God was not to him a hazy light breaking through the tangle of the evolutionary undergrowth, nor a blinding brilliancy in the highest place of the heavens. God was to him the magnificent old man depicted in his dark and extraordinary illustrations of 'Job,' the old man with the monstrous muscles, the mild stern eyebrows, the long smooth silver hair and beard" (149).

Many years ago, when reading C.S. Lewis, I came across the idea that spirit is more solid than what we see and touch and call matter. Lewis was speaking about Christ entering the room after his resurrection, "the doors being closed." He said that this was possible because now his spiritual body was more solid than the wall. We think of spirit as some kind of gaseous substance, like a cloud or mist. It is just the opposite: spirit is more solid than matter.

The main point that Chesterton wants us to understand is that: "Blake held that Deity is more solid than humanity. He held that what we call the ideal is not only more beautiful but more actual than the real" (149).

Think of solid substances such as iron and stone. The God who surrounds us is infinitely more solid than any of those substances. What we often call the absence of God is really his gentleness. He is protecting us from experiencing too much of his reality. If he is the Essence of fire, strength, power, and so on, and this Essence is surrounding us at every moment, we need his protection from himself. We could not stand too much of his reality. Remember as children how gently we held a soap bubble in our hands, to keep it from breaking. That's how gently God must hold us, lest we break.

This solidity of the ideal, of spirit, is "the idea of ideas" in Blake (156). And because he encompasses this kernel of truth, Chesterton has some very high praise for him, despite all the convolutions of his thinking:

No man had harder dogmas; no one insisted more that religion must have theology. The Everlasting Gospel was far from being a simple gospel. Blake had succeeded in inventing in the course of about ten years as tangled and interdependent a system of theology as the Catholic Church has accumulated in two thousand. (156)

When considering the unorthodox thinkers of history, we often concentrate on their errors. Chesterton says that historians need to exercise their imagination in order to consider "what might have been." What if gnostics such as Marcion, Arius, Voltaire, and Blake had been converted to the orthodox Church? What an intellectual enrichment they would have provided to the faithful. On the other hand, it might be pointed out, what if we had lost Augustine, Bernard, Catherine of Siena, and Teresa of Avila to false mysticism!

And, horror of horrors, what if we had lost Chesterton to the spiritualism and gnosticism of the early part of this century! I am sure that he, aware of his human frailty, would have heartily endorsed St. Paul's conviction that "there, but for the grace of God, go I." Thank God for giving Chesterton the humility to believe more in the light of the Church than in his own inner light. Imagine his great mind and mystical gifts turned against the Church!

Blake, then, was a tragic mystic, when all is said and done. He was, for all that, sincere and courageous, a talented poet and artist. Some of his early visions were probably from the Holy Spirit. The tragedy was that he did not ask the Catholic Church about them. She could have told him about Ezekiel and angels in the trees. But he was cut off from this great tradition. Being uneducated in philosophy or theology, he was easily deluded and misguided. Blake is the prime modern exponent of

> a return of mysticism without the Christianity. Mysticism itself [in the false sense] has returned, with all its moons and twilights, its talismans and spells, and brought with it seven devils worse that itself.[6]

The problem, Chesterton remarks pointedly, is that now we have the devils without the Redeemer.[7] Now, too, we have visions without a Church to interpret them.

Nevertheless, for all his gnosticism, Blake retained some important scraps of the Western mystical tradition. Especially did he believe that forgiveness was of the essence of Christ's heart. We have every reason to hope that he himself obtained it.

6 *The Everlasting Man*, 177.
7 Ibid., 170.

Little Lamb, who made thee? Dost thou know who made thee? Little Lamb, I'll tell thee, Little Lamb, I'll tell thee. He is called by thy name, for he calls himself a Lamb. He is meek, & he is mild; He became a little child. I, a child, & thou a lamb, we are called by his name.[8]

Blake believed, as well, in the book of Revelation, where the Lamb is the temple of the New Jerusalem and its lamp:

> Then the angel showed me the river of the water of life, as clear as crystal, flowing from the throne of God and of the Lamb down the middle of the great street of the city. On each side of the river stood the tree of life, bearing twelve crops of fruit, yielding its fruit every month. And the leaves of the tree are for the healing of the nations. No longer will there be any curse. The throne of God and of the Lamb will be in the city, and his servant will serve him. They will see his face, and his name will be on their foreheads. (Rev. 22:1–4)

All the mystics of all ages and traditions had some experience of the Presence, desired to see his face, and tried to communicate what they saw. We have every reason to hope that now they see what they longed for. The Buddha and John of the Cross and Blake and Chesterton will one day be at the Lamb's feast, enjoying ecstatic conversations about the Presence they behold. And their spirits will be very solid.

Towards the end of his life, on BBC radio, Chesterton quoted Blake favorably: "Blake said very truly, a tear is an intellectual thing." When men are gathered around the heavenly wedding table between the Bride and the Lamb, "[God] will wipe every tear from their eyes" (Rev. 21:4). Only joy will be there, and it will be the most solid reality of all.

---

8 William Blake, *The Penguin Poets* (New York: Penguin, 2005), 22.

10

Tolstoy, The Fraticelli, Huxley

We turn now to a few mystical tumblers who, in Chesterton's view, failed in some ways to arrive at a balanced mysticism, having landed on their heads.

Tolstoy: Fanatical Mystic

Chesterton was already thinking about mystics and mysticism in 1902 when writing about Tolstoy. The great man was still alive, and many people were considering him a mystic, as some still do. My Webster Dictionary gives this one line biographical sketch of Tolstoy: "1828–1910. Russ. nov., philos., & mystic." Tolstoy was writing books on the Kingdom of God, and preaching that love is the answer to all problems. Chesterton must have scandalized many as a brash and ignorant young man when he wrote:

> A great modern writer [Tolstoy] erases theology altogether, denies the validity of the Scriptures and the Churches alike, forms a purely ethical theory that love should be the instrument of reform, and ends by maintaining that we have no right to strike a man if he is torturing a child before our eyes. He goes on. He develops a theory of the mind and the emotions, which might be held by the most rigid atheists, and he ends by maintaining that the sexual relation out of which all humanity has come, is not only not moral, but is positively not natural. This is fanaticism as it has been and as it will always be.[1]

---

1 Quoted in *The Chesterton Review*, Feb., 1994, 7.

Chesterton discovered that genuine mystics had a balance and a realism which people like Tolstoy lacked. Joan of Arc, for example:

> Joan of Arc was not stuck at the cross-roads, either by rejecting all the paths like Tolstoy, or by accepting them all like Nietzsche. Joan had in her all that was true either in Tolstoy or Nietzsche, all that was tolerable in either of them. We know that she was not afraid of an army, while Nietzsche, for all we know, was afraid of a cow. Tolstoy only praised the peasant; she was the peasant. Nietzsche only praised the warrior; she was the warrior. It was impossible that the thought should not cross my mind that she and her faith had perhaps some secret of moral unity and utility that has been lost.[2]

Already then, as early as 1905 with the publication of *Heretics,* there appears what will become the great theme of *Orthodoxy* (1908). A passage like the following leads one to suppose that *Orthodoxy* might have been partially inspired by Chesterton's horrified reaction to this great and internationally known writer at the turn of the century:

> The truth is that Tolstoy, with his immense genius, with his colossal faith, with his vast fearlessness and vast knowledge of life, is deficient in one faculty and one faculty alone. He is not a mystic: therefore he has a tendency to go mad. Men talk of the extravagances and frenzies that have been produced by mysticism: they are a mere drop in the bucket. In the main, and from the beginning of time, mysticism has kept men sane. The thing that has driven them mad was logic. It is significant that, with all that has been said about the excitability of poets, only one English poet ever went mad, and he went mad from a logical system of theology. He was Cowper, and his poetry retarded his insanity for many years. So poetry, in which Tolstoy is deficient, has always been a tonic and sanative thing. The only thing that

---

2 *Heretics* (New York: Dodd, Mead & Co., 1925), 79.

has kept the race of men from the mad extremes of the convent and the pirate-galley, 'the night-club and the lethal chamber,' has been mysticism—the belief that logic is misleading, and that things are not what they seem.[3]

Here he defines mysticism as a kind of poetry, equating it also with an attitude that goes beyond logic and is open to mystery.

In Chapter X of *Heretics*, entitled "On Sandals and Simplicity," this perverse mystical attitude on the part of Tolstoy is further elaborated. This chapter contains several of what I would call Chesterton's principles of mysticism as understood by him at this time of his life.

First, mere logic, in matters where people are striving for holiness or for some ideal of human existence, often leads people astray. Basically, he says the Tolstoyans spend so much time thinking about how to be simple, that they not only cease to be truly simple, but come up with ideas which are quite untrue. "They would make us simple in unimportant things, but complex in the important things" (136). Giving up meat or wearing sandals or some such Spartan regime is not the essence of simplicity:

> It does not so very much matter whether a man eats a grilled tomato or a plain tomato; it does very much matter whether he eats a plain tomato with a grilled mind. The only kind of simplicity worth preserving is the simplicity of the heart, the simplicity which accepts and enjoys. There may be a reasonable doubt as to what system preserves this; there can be no doubt that a system of simplicity destroys it. There is more simplicity in the man who eats caviar on impulse than in the man who eats grape-nuts on principle. (136)

What must be preserved is what he calls, in a beautiful phrase, "the virginity of spirit, which enjoys with astonishment and fear" (139). He doesn't say that the enjoyment of good things is the only method of preserving this virginity of spirit. Thus, he does

---

3 Ibid., 7. Following page references refer to this book.

not discount the legitimate asceticism of the saints. "But I will have nothing to do with simplicity which lacks the fear, the astonishment, and the joy alike" (139).

He sees in the spontaneous intuitions of the child a sure guide to this "virginity of spirit":

> The child is, indeed, in these, and many other matters, the best guide. And in nothing is the child so righteously child-like, in nothing does he exhibit more accurately the sounder order of simplicity, than in the fact that he sees everything with a simple pleasure, even the complex things. (139)

The child, in his wonder at things, does not distinguish between natural and man-made things. His is an intuition of being, of the *it-is-thereness* of things: whatever is *there* is astounding:

> The false kind of naturalness harps always on the distinction between the natural and the artificial. The higher kind of naturalness ignores that distinction. To the child the tree and the lamp-post are as natural and as artificial as each other; or rather, neither of them is natural but both are supernatural. For both are splendid and unexplained. (139)

I find quite interesting his point that for the child (and for the mystic?) everything is supernatural. It is "supernatural," in his view, because it is drawn forth from nothingness. Everything is equally astounding *just for being.*[4] The following could well stand as a summary of Chesterton's whole view of reality:

> In this matter, then, as in all the other matters treated in this book, our main conclusion is that it is a fundamental point of view, a philosophy or religion which is needed, and not any change in habit or social routine. The things we need most for immediate practical purposes are all abstractions. We need a right view of the human lot, a right view of the human society; and if we were living eagerly and angrily in

---

4 "It is not how things are in the world that is mystical, but that it exists" (Ludwig Wittgenstein). Quoted by Edward T. Oakes, "Philosophy in an Old Key," *First Things*, Dec., 2000, 29.

the enthusiasm of those things, we should, *ipso facto*, be living simply. 'But seek first the kingdom of God and His righteousness, and all these things shall be added unto you.' Those amazing words are not only extraordinarily good, practical politics; they are also superlatively good hygiene. The one supreme way of making all those processes go right, the processes of health, and strength, and grace, and beauty, the one and only way of making certain of their accuracy, is to think about something else. (141)

He will say later on in *Orthodoxy* that a healthy person does not think about his health. A person, for example, who plans to take a trip around the world, must be very healthy indeed, or he would not be able to concentrate on planning such an enterprise, much less do it. In such a case, good health is simply a given. Applying this metaphor to the realm of the mystical, Chesterton is against people being preoccupied with an interior system of mysticism. If they are thus preoccupied, it often becomes a block to their ability to experience reality as it is. The interior system becomes a "mystification" which hinders true spontaneity and wonder.

For the thing called 'taking thought,' the thing for which the best modern word is 'rationalizing,' is in its nature, inapplicable to all plain and urgent things. Men take thought and ponder rationalistically, touching remote things—things that only theoretically matter, such as the transit to Venus. But only at their peril can men rationalize about so practical a matter as health. (141)

It could be added that only at their peril do men rationalize about a mystical theory. It would be bad for their spiritual health.

The Fraticelli

Chesterton offers more reflections on false mystics when he treats in *St. Francis* of the sect called the Fraticelli. When I first read Chesterton's treatment of them, it struck me as rather harsh. Not knowing a great deal about them, I set about doing some research, trying to relate Chesterton's estimation of them with the historical realities. In examining this issue of the Fraticelli, I will look at Chesterton's evaluation first of all, and then some comments from the historian. Chesterton describes them in this way:

> A sect that came to be called the Fraticelli declared themselves the true sons of St. Francis and broke away from the compromises of Rome in favour of what they would have called the complete programme of Assisi. In a very little while these loose Franciscans began to look as ferocious as Flagellants. They launched new and violent vetoes; they denounced marriage; that is, they denounced mankind. In the name of the most human of saints they declared war upon humanity. They did not perish particularly through being persecuted; many of them were eventually persuaded; and the unpersuadable rump of them that remained without producing anything in the least calculated to remind anybody of the real St. Francis. What was the matter with these people was that they were mystics; mystics and nothing else but mystics; mystics and not Catholics; mystics and not Christians; mystics and not men. They rotted away because, in the most exact sense, they would not listen to reason. And St. Francis, however wild and romantic his gyrations might appear to many, always hung on to reason by one invisible and indestructible hair. (228)

The first thing that struck me about this passage was Chesterton's emphatic reiteration of the word "mystic" without any qualification, obviously in a pejorative sense: "They were mystics, mystics and nothing else but mystics, mystics and not men." As I remarked earlier, he probably did not agree with some of what is even considered to be orthodox Christian mysticism; certainly he couldn't identify with a lot of it; and shied away from aspects of it as uncongenial. I suspect he found too much mystification in many mystics, too many mirrors upon mirrors upon mirrors.

It may be asked whether Chesterton was capable of a sort of intellectual disdain for an anonymous group of people. He did in fact go so far as to say one time that he hated individualists more than he hated Communists. Without a doubt this was an instance of typical Chestertonian hyperbole, used rhetorically to draw attention to his fervent ideological convictions. I, for one, do not believe he hated any particular individualist or Communist. It is fairly certain, however, that he did have certain intellectual antipathies, directed towards given groups of people on account of what they stood for.

His comments in the above-quoted passage about the Fraticelli contains a strongly negative attitude towards much of what goes by the name of mysticism. He does not treat the Fraticelli with any of his usual delicacy and understanding. They are total blackguards. Nevertheless, it must be asked whether this was true historically. Here is what the scholars say:

> Besides some views shared with other and earlier movements, notably the Waldensians, such as the beliefs that to take an oath was mortal sin, and that the sinful priest was powerless to administer the sacraments, the *Fraticelli's* characteristic major errors are defined [in the Bull *Gloriosam Ecclesiam*]: the Roman Church is the Carnal Church, wealthy and depraved, ruled by authority; whereas they themselves are the Spiritual Church, poor and virtuous, ruled on the basis of spiritual merit; true authority, and the power of the sacraments, has passed from the first to the second; and in the second resides the Gospel of Christ.[5]

Chesterton's criticism of these errors, in which he explains what could have happened if they had not been opposed, is accurate. Here again he is talking about the Fraticelli:

> Every heresy has been an effort to narrow the Church. If the Franciscan movement had turned into a new religion, it would after all have been a narrow religion. In so far as it did turn here and there into a heresy, it was a narrow heresy. It did what heresy always does; it set the mood against the mind. The mood was indeed originally the good and glori-

5 Nimmo, op. cit., 191.

ous mood of the great St. Francis, but it was not the whole mind of God or even of man. And it is a fact that the mood itself degenerated, as the mood turned into a monomania. (227)

The Fraticelli movement encompassed a broad spectrum of men, including the very sincere and zealous, fanatics, sexual anti-nomians, and some who pillaged and destroyed a few convents of the Order. Many were honestly and wholeheartedly trying to live the rule precisely as St. Francis had done. They saw the subsequent evolution of the Order as a betrayal of the Gospel. Nimmo explains what happened:

> Placing this development in the historical context, we might say that, in his compact with Francis, Innocent III had appeared to promise the Christian world that the total 'life of the Gospel,' as literally construed, would be realized through the saint's followers; the subsequent evolution of his Order, directed by Innocent III's successors, progressively falsified that promise. The error of the poverty radicals was to see the fact as a 'betrayal of the Gospel,' and tantamount to heresy, but the fact cannot be gainsaid: during the 13th century there *was* a derogation from the evangelical ideal lived, with total commitment, by Francis himself, and the papal office largely directed it.[6]

I cite this, not to get involved in the historical Franciscan controversy, but to allow a bit of mercy and understanding for mystics who go off the rails, or fall on their heads in their mystical tumbling. Chesterton had to come down hard on heretical moods which destroy the fabric of orthodoxy. But we can most certainly sympathize with people who have become overpowered by the mystical experience, and have failed to land on their feet. As Chesterton himself said, "the mood was indeed originally the good and glorious mood of the great St. Francis."

The Fraticelli could not obey the Church because their pseudo-mystical intuitions told them that they were right and the

6 Ibid., 199.

Church was wrong. But in the spirit of the saintly Gilbert, I ask for a moment of silent prayer on behalf of all the misguided pseudo-mystics. Many of them were zealous and sincere, but not humble enough to obey. Their mystical tumbling made them dizzy, and they did not land on the firm ground of orthodoxy. They burrowed deeply into the divine darkness, but did not come out far enough to see the light of Christ shining on the face of his Spouse, the Church. Misguided zealots are not to be imitated. Still, one wonders whether the Lord will not judge them more leniently than those who are steeped in apathy, indifference, and fearful conformity in regards to the errors of the day. For all its pitfalls, enthusiasm has its attractive facets, while apathy, God knows, has none at all.

At the very end of *St. Francis*, Chesterton gives what I would call "Directives for Fostering Genuine Mystics." They apply to Francis and to all the orthodox mystics of the Church. In fact, it is only by using these directives that the Church Herself is able to know if men and women "drunk with the Spirit" are genuine or not:

> The great saint was sane; and with the very sound of the word sanity, as at a deeper chord struck upon a harp, we come back to something that was indeed deeper than everything about him that seemed an almost elfish eccentricity. He was not a mere eccentric because he was always turning towards the centre and heart of the maze; he took the queerest and most zig-zag short cuts through the wood, but he was always going home. He was not only far too humble to be an heresiarch, but he was far too human to desire to be an extremist, in the sense of an exile at the ends of the earth. The sense of humour which salts all the stories of his escapades alone prevented him from ever hardening into the solemnity of sectarian self-righteousness. He was by nature ready to admit that he was wrong.[7]

---

7 *St. Francis of Assisi* (New York: George H. Doran Co., 1924), 228–29.

A Contrast in Mysticism: Huxley and Chesterton

It was several years after my own reflections on Chesterton's mysticism, and well into this present study, that I came upon Anthony Grist's article, "A Contrast in Mysticism."[8] It is always a delight to come across someone who agrees with you! And it does not seem to me that I am reading my own theory of Chesterton's mysticism into that of Grist. Whatever the case, let the reader judge. I do, however, think that Grist has reached the same conclusions about the essence of Chesterton's mysticism as I have:

> And yet there is a kind of mysticism in Chesterton's work. It is manifested as a heightened awareness of the glorious otherness of things. It was almost certainly a natural gift, but he developed it into something like a philosophy in response to the spiritual crisis of his youth.
>
> Chesterton's own kind of mysticism was the re-discovery that 'at the back of our brains, so to speak, there was a forgotten blaze or burst of astonishment at our own existence'; and, so far as one can judge, this 'burst of astonishment' never left him. It is much more than an idea: it is a way of seeing and of feeling that puts him in the very English tradition of such born mystics as Thomas Traherne, William Wordsworth and Francis Thompson. In this tradition, the works of God do not veil their Creator, they proclaim Him.[9]

To Grist's "he developed it into something like a philosophy," I would substitute—as is the thesis of this book—that sometime during his life he received a truly mystical grace of always being aware in a supernatural way of the "burst of astonishment at the back of our brains."

Aldous Huxley is one of my favorite biographers of religious personalities. I have read both his *Gray Eminence* and *The Devils of Loudun* several times. They are veritable gold mines of insight into true and false Christian mysticism. The subtitle of *Gray Emi-*

---

8 *The Chesterton Review,* Vol. XVI, No.3–4, Aug.–Nov., 1990, 229–237.
9 Ibid., 236.

nence is "A Study in Religion and Politics." The book is a fascinating account of how a very generous and sincere mystic can become unglued by the intensity of his religious convictions, and thus lose the harmony and balance of the orthodox Catholic vision in his relationship to the two worlds of heaven and earth. Instead, Father Joseph became a "mere mystic," to use Chesterton's phrase.

I highly recommend Huxley's book, inasmuch as Chesterton was also involved in politics, to the extent, at least, of reflecting on how a believer should view political issues in the light of the Christian faith. In this respect, Chesterton could be considered a very "Bright Eminence." Like his great countryman Thomas More, Chesterton knew that there were lines one must not cross over in one's attempts to foster the kingdom of God upon the earth.

According to Huxley, at least, Father Joseph was carried away by his religious enthusiasm. Chesterton, for his part, considered enthusiasm one of the greatest of virtues. Literally, this word, which comes from the Greek, means "in God." The trick is to keep one's mystical feet on the Ground of Being that is God, in the midst of the worldly turmoil of politics. Father Joseph became ungrounded. He lost his moorings.

Huxley's work is a profound examination of the limits of religion in politics, especially in the case of mystics who participate in politics. His tenth chapter, "Politics and Religion," coupled with Chesterton's own Catholic views on politics, would make a fascinating comparative study.

All the same, it is sad to discover that all of Huxley's researches into Christian mysticism, as evidenced by the works cited above, did not lead him to Christ. At the end of his life he opted for Eastern modes of thought. Referring to *The Perennial Philosophy,* another of Huxley's books, Grist explains that it is

> an impressive, lucid work, which shows admirable mastery of a great range of materials. Huxley quotes from Hindu and Buddhist scriptures, from Chinese poets and Sufi aphorists. He avoids the Bible, arguing that over-familiarity has

dulled its impact, but he quotes widely from other Christian authorities.[10]

Grist says that Huxley's mystical philosophy appears complex and esoteric only because it is not really a philosophy at all. Huxley pinpoints what all Christian mystics would agree upon: that God is unknowable; that language is inadequate in speaking about God; that God is not "out there" but "is," and penetrates all reality, and so on. But, unfortunately, he allows these agreed upon positions to lead him into what I could call "the perennial soup," the mistake of mixing all reality together indiscriminately and saying that all mystical experiences are at bottom the same.

Quoting a passage from a Father Brown story, "The Dagger with Wings," Grist says it is a pretty fair parody of *The Perennial Philosophy*:

'You do believe it,' he said. 'You do believe everything. We all believe everything, even when we deny everything. The deniers believe. The unbelievers believe. Don't you feel in your heart that these contradictions do not really contradict: that there is a cosmos that contains them all? The soul goes round upon a wheel of stars and all things return. Good and evil go round in a wheel that is one thing, and not many. Do you not realise in your heart, do you not believe behind all your beliefs, that there is but one reality and we are its shadows; and that all things are but aspects of one thing: a centre where men melt into Man and Man into God.' Father Brown merely comments that 'it is the religion of rascals.'[11]

As a result of his own pilgrimage to Rome, Chesterton would come to say:

Christianity is the religion of the Resurrection; in which it differs, for instance, from Buddhism, which is the religion of the Recurrence or Return, which in practice means little more than what men of science used to call the Conservation of Energy. That is, the idea that every elemental force

10 Ibid., 231.
11 Ibid., 233.

or expression returns in some form; but the form does not return. Nothing but the Christian Creed has ever had the audacity to assert that a thing will actually recover its identity because it will recover its form.[12]

I agree with Grist that Chesterton probably disagreed with some Christian mysticism:

It is also true that he [Chesterton] had little sympathy with that mystical tradition within Catholicism which, in Huxley's view, is in agreement with the mysticism of the East. The Catholic writers whom Huxley values most, St. John of the Cross, St. Francis de Sales, Francois Fenelon, scarcely figure at all in Chesterton's account of Catholic history, spirituality, and thought.[13]

I have already remarked on the reason for his possible lack of interest in Julian of Norwich. The writings of another of his compatriots, the author of *The Cloud of Unknowing*, would, I suspect, have been too cloudy for his taste:

This darkness and this cloud is, howsoever thou dost, betwixt thee and thy God. And therefore shape thee to bide in this darkness as long as thou mayest, evermore crying after Him that thou lovest. For if ever thou shalt feel Him or see Him as it may be here, it behoveth always to be in this cloud and this darkness.[14]

Chesterton, I'm sure, would have bowed before the mystic author's experience and would not have presumed to judge him. But he also might have believed that the unknown author had entered a lofty cloud and could not find his way back to earth. It would have been too Eastern for Chesterton. He wanted the mystic's insight to illuminate the earth.

Chesterton did not see much good in Eastern thought. This, however, is an understandable attitude, given the period he lived

12 *The Resurrection of Rome* (London: Hodder and Stoughton, Ltd, 1934), 119–120.
13 Grist, 236.
14 *Cloud of Unknowing*, iii.

in. He was encountering, and fighting against, a great deal of pseudo-Eastern thought in the form of Theosophy, which was championed by people like Madame Blavatsky. He himself had dabbled in this and had had an experience of its darkness:

> The Theosophical initiate strips away the veils of illusion one by one in order to discover, as the last of them is twitched off, that they have been concealing nothing at all. 'It isn't a very cheerful philosophy that everything is illusion,' said W.B. Yeats—and Chesterton agreed.[15]

Chesterton, of course, never had access to the many more accurate and intelligent modern studies which seek a greater clarification of the relationship between Christian and Eastern thought. For all that, Chesterton still serves as a penetrating and important guide into the real differences between the two worlds.

Grist's conclusion is significant for my purposes. Alluding to one of Huxley's last books, *The Doors of Perception*, he says:

> To use a phrase of Blake's which Huxley liked, the doors of perception are cleansed. The cleansed perception which was Chesterton's birthright became for Huxley a state to be artificially induced as, in the last decade of his life, his hunger for mystical experience led him into experimentation with psychedelic drugs.[16]

Huxley was a great man, a fighter, and a seeker after truth, the sort of man Chesterton always respected, even when he deprecated his views. It was a great tragedy, however, that Huxley, who could have sought his mystical experiences through faith in Christ, chose instead to induce them through drugs. Since mystical experiences cannot be willed, he would, as a Christian, have needed an extraordinary infusion of grace to have them. Still, the first traces of this grace, the first intimations of our immortal destiny, come through that wonder of wonders, the sacrament of baptism, which gives us our birthright in the Kingdom.

15 Ibid., 232.
16 Ibid., 236–237.

There are, to be sure, aberrations in Christian mysticism. These are, however, a drop in the bucket compared to its many successes. It was the American philosopher, William Hocking, who said that mystics such as Teresa of Avila and John of the Cross are worth all the failures of Christian mysticism, because they have shown us the splendid heights of human existence.

Chesterton had the grace to see that the doors of perception can be cleansed through grace. We do not need the elaborate techniques of the East. When Jesus was asked to teach his disciples to pray, the whole context of his instructions presumes that prayer is both possible and available to all. He did not give his disciples an intricate methodology and technique when he taught them to pray. He simply said, *"When you pray, say, Our Father."* Chesterton is a wise guide to the mystical spirituality which is possible and available to all of God's children.

The Lord can use any aspect of his creation, and any truth of the faith, in order to ignite an awareness of his Presence. Thus, by a touch of his Finger (which St. Irenaeus calls the Holy Spirit), God can illuminate one's whole life, whether it be through a powerful experience of Jesus in the Blessed Sacrament, Christ's presence in a poor person (Martin of Tours), the starry heavens, the timelessness of a rock (Teilhard de Chardin), an awareness of his indwelling Presence (Elizabeth of the Trinity), or the solitude of a desert (St. Anthony)—to name just a few of the means God can use. This one touch, moreover, can be so strong that one then experiences his Presence everywhere. It's like an experience of first love, lighting up the whole world in its warm glow.

The danger is that, if a person is not obedient to the faith and teaching of the Church, this experience can distort and minimize the other truths of the faith, even obliterate some of them altogether. Many mystics, both within and outside the Church, have been thrown off their feet by their powerful experiences. They run the risk of becoming too eccentric, which means, quite literally, "to be outside the center." And although Chesterton says somewhere that most of reality is eccentric, he would be talking about the reality that the Creator created. I'm sure he would agree that there is a wrong way to be eccentric. He was eccentric himself, but in the extreme center!

The truth or object which God uses to manifest his Presence can be misunderstood and become one's personal center in a way that distorts the balance of orthodoxy. Chesterton's mystical intuition of the *it-is-thereness* of things and of the Presence shining forth in the astounding reality of creation, does not become the center of his faith. The center of his faith, as with all true Christian mystics, is Jesus Christ. But the Lord, in some definite way, ignited Chesterton's awareness of the Presence through the medium of creation. Nature did not become the center of his life: Jesus Christ remained his Center. The Lord used the goodness of creation to lead Chesterton to the One whom Jesus said, "No one is good but God alone."

PART IV

THE SONS OF GOD SHOUTING FOR JOY

11

Job's Riddling God:
Chesterton's Consoler?

Several times throughout this book I have touched upon the severe crisis that Chesterton went through in his early manhood. In his Introduction to *The Man Who Was Thursday*, Garry Wills writes about the novel:

> The tale is not an idle play with symbols. It gets its urgency and compression from the fact that it is the most successful embodiment of the seminal experience in Chesterton's life, his young *mystical* brush with insanity—his depression and near-suicide as an art student in the decadent nineties.[1]

If Chesterton was the recipient of a mystical grace, it could not have come through a mere philosophical inquiry into the nature of reality. Chesterton is often seen as a Pollyanna type, rollicking through life without any real experience of suffering. This is far from being the case. Whatever the pains of his later life—the death of his brother, his own heroic battles against the forces of decay in the society of his time—there is ample evidence to indicate that he did experience a very severe dark night in his early years. Many writers have depicted this period in sufficient detail. I only wish to allude to it briefly here in order to suggest that *it may have been during these years he was rescued by a mystical grace.*

---

1 (New York: Sheed and Ward, 1975). Denis Conlon says that "One might argue over the 'near-suicide' while admitting, as the dedicatory verses tell us, that 'This is a tale of those old fears,' the 'blind spiritual suicide' of which Chesterton speaks in his *Autobiography*" (*The Chesterton Review*, Vol. II, No.1, Fall–Winter, 1975, 79).

Could this have been the hole that he descended to its depths until he finally started to go up, up?

Leo Hetzler says that Chesterton's early poem (1892?), "Hymn to the Spirit of Religion," reveals that Chesterton was, at that time, not sure if the Spirit behind everything was *"sweet or bitter"*:

> The shapes and the forms of worship
> wherein the divine was seen,
> Are shattered and cast away on the fields
> of the things that have been.
> A terrible stir of change and waking
> through [out] all the land,
> Till we know what things to believe,
> or what knowledge be near at hand.
> Therefore I turn unto thee, the nameless
> infinite [one],
> Mother of all the creeds that dawn
> and dwell and are gone.
> Voice in the heart of man, imperative,
> changeless, blind,
> That calls to the building of faiths
> through the ages of all mankind
> Fathomless mystical impulse, that is
> and forever has been. . . .
> Thou art more than all the faiths,
> or false or true that befall,
> For thou art the unseen force
> that is under and shapeth all. . . .
> But a doom that is sweet or bitter
> has bound us forever to thee.[2]

There is an oft-quoted passage from his *Autobiography* where he speaks of his early crisis. It certainly reveals someone in the throes of personal chaos:

2 Quoted in *The Chesterton Review,* "Chesterton's Teen-Age Writings," Vol. II, No.1, 75.

I had thought my way back to thought itself. It is a dreadful thing to do; for it may lead to thinking that there is nothing but thought. At this time I did not very clearly distinguish between dreaming and waking, not only as a mood, but as a metaphysical doubt. I felt as if everything might be a dream. It was as if I had myself projected the universe from within, with all its trees and stars; and that is so near to the notion of being God that it is manifestly even nearer to going mad.[3]

While we do not know exactly when Chesterton's dark night occurred or how long it lasted, Noel O'Donoghue beautifully sums up my own opinion that a truly mystical grace was given to Chesterton during this time. He refers to Chesterton's "mysticism of the ordinary," saying that it could not have been born out of the "optimism of an expansive personality, of heartiness and good fellowship." Rather, it is "the optimism of the mystic":

The mystic is the man who is illuminated by a light, warmed by a fire, strengthened by a power that is somehow from beyond or from outside himself. At least this is one way of describing the mystic, a way that can find ample support from some of the greatest mystics of west and east. Usually the mystic has suffered greatly and has passed through something that may be called a conversion experience. It is not difficult to find a basis for this formula in Chesterton's own account of his boyhood and early manhood. He came out of great darkness into marvelous light.

The darkness was the darkness of the alien and uncanny, of a paradise utterly lost, of limitless desert and unending night. The experience might also be an alien land of strange inhuman inhabitants. Yet the voyage ended in a landfall in his own land, among his own people.

Was the voyage then unnecessary? By no means. It was necessary to go away in order to return. It was essential to be utterly deprived of the light of common day in order to receive this higher light that was yet but a recovery of the

3 *Autobiography,* 92.

light of childhood. It was as if he had to turn round in order to share the light in its source.

This experience was also warmth and power, infusing and energising his natural genius. That inner glory which his writing expressed in a thousand ways, was also the source of that vigour and skill with which he expressed it.[4]

No doubt many thoughts and experiences prepared for this grace. The one I wish to highlight here is the influence of the Book of Job or, more precisely, of Job's God. Job's "riddling God" (Wills), whom Chesterton encountered in his dark night, was one of the factors which prepared Chesterton's mind and heart for his mystical enlightenment.

It is Garry Wills' opinion that the Book of Job was a life-long preoccupation of Chesterton's, and that references to it "are everywhere" in *The Man Who Was Thursday*.[5] He also claims that Job was the companion of Chesterton's troubled years and that *Thursday* is the description of those years of pain and confusion and searching. A fair expanse of years lies between Chesterton's bout with lunacy in his twenties and his *Introduction to the Book of Job* (1907) where he spelled out, in a more prosaic fashion, his thoughts about Job.[6]

> This seems to me his most important essay, written on the book that most profoundly influenced him all his life. Composed just before *The Man Who Was Thursday*, it could almost stand as a commentary on the novel.[7]

Without trying to determine how much of the *Introduction* was part of his thinking during the dark years, I will simply draw on the *Introduction* to sketch out how the Book of Job consoled Chesterton. In those years of darkness he went mostly to the Old Testament for answers. In his Notebooks, moreover, there are several imitations of Job's speeches.

The Book of Job would have appealed to him for many rea-

4 *The Chesterton Review*, "Chesterton's Marvelous Boyhood," VI, No. 1, 106.
5 *Chesterton, Man and Mask* (New York: Sheed & Ward, 1961).
6 *G. K. C. as M. C.* and *Selected Essays*, 34–52.
7 Wills, 221.

sons, not least of which would have been its consummate art, which made it "the literary masterpiece of the Wisdom movement."[8] Many scholars claim it is the most beautifully written book in the whole bible. It contains a dramatic story too, with vivid scenes, which range from Satan's roaming about the earth, on to the destruction of Job's goods and family, then to the very lively discussions with his so-called "friends," and finally to the superb speeches of God at the end. The whole book would have appealed to Chesterton's story-telling sense.

According to Chesterton, Job is the first biblical character about whom it can be said that he emerges as a distinct person. The first part of the bible is mostly about the personality of God, so much so that Chesterton is led to assert that "God is properly the only character in the Old Testament." In comparison with God, the human players in the Old Testament are like saws and hammers in the hands of the carpenter:

> The main characteristic remains the sense not merely that God is stronger than man, but that He means more, that He knows better what He is doing, that compared with Him we have something of the vagueness, the unreason, and the vagrancy of the beasts that perish.[9]

Then The Book of Job comes along, "the most interesting of modern books," as Chesterton piquantly puts it. Job is the first to ask questions of God, the same questions that Chesterton was asking in his darkness:

> The Book of Job stands definitely alone because the Book of Job definitely asks, 'But what is the purpose of God?' Is it worth the sacrifice even of our miserable humanity? Of course it is easy enough to wipe out our own paltry wills for the sake of a will that is grander and kinder. But is it grander and kinder? Let God use His tools; let God break His tools.

---

8 New Jerusalem Bible, 753.

9 Introduction to the Book of Job in G. K. C. as M. C, 40. Page numbers in this section are from this Introduction unless otherwise noted.

But what is He doing and what are they being broken for? (41)

These are also philosophical questions, and Chesterton himself was in the throes of philosophical problems. "The first of the intellectual beauties of the Book of Job is that it is all concerned with this desire to know the actuality; the desire to know what is, and not merely what seems" (42). *Impressionism* was woven out of what seems, which is precisely what Chesterton was battling.

Chesterton doubts if the words "optimist" or "pessimist" mean anything, although, according to their superficial meaning, Job's supposed friends are pessimists, and Job himself is an optimist. Job's friends do not really believe in the goodness of God: "All that they really believe is not that God is good but that God is so strong that it is much more judicious to call Him good" (42).

Chesterton was a good person, like Job. Like Job, he had count-less questions he hurled at God. Like Job, he was not hurling these questions at the Unknown out of rage or anger or contempt or skepticism:

Job does it in the spirit in which a wife might demand an explanation from her husband whom she really respected. He remonstrates with his Maker because he is proud of his Maker. He even speaks of the Almighty as his enemy, but he never doubts, at the back of his mind, that his enemy has some kind of a case which he does not understand. In a fine and famous blasphemy he says, 'Oh, that mine adversary had written a book!' It never really occurs to him that it could possibly be a bad book. He is anxious to be convinced, that is, he thinks that God could convince him. In short, we may say again that if the word optimist means anything (which I doubt) Job is an optimist. He shakes the pillars of the world and strikes insanely at the heavens; he lashes the stars, but it is not to silence them; it is to make them speak. (43)

This is, no doubt, a description of Chesterton's own period of confusion and anguish. His over-sized brain was churning out questions and doubts at a rapid and maniacal speed. But there's nothing wrong with doubting:

It is the root and reason of the fact that men who have religious faith have also philosophic doubt, like Cardinal Newman, Mr. Balfour, or Mr. Mallock. These are the small streams of the delta; the Book of Job is the first great cataract that creates the river. (46)

Nobody could have told Chesterton to stop doubting. This is not the way to satisfy questioning minds. From his own experience he learned that

In dealing with the arrogant asserter of doubt, it is not the right method to tell him to stop doubting. It is rather the right method to tell him to go on doubting, to doubt a little more, to doubt every day newer and wilder things in the universe until at last, by some strange enlightenment, he may begin to doubt himself. (46)

This is the place where Chesterton himself arrived: he began to doubt himself, that is, the ability of his own rational powers to completely understand reality. It is the realization of this limitation which led Job—and Chesterton—to the frontiers of the religious sphere:

The other great fact which, taken together makes the whole work religious instead of merely philosophical, is that other great surprise which makes Job suddenly satisfied with the mere presentation of something impenetrable. Verbally speaking the enigmas of Jehovah seem darker and more desolate than the enigmas of Job; yet Job was comfortless before the speech of Jehovah and is comforted after it. He has been told nothing, but he feels the terrible and tingling atmosphere of something which is too good to be told. The refusal of God to explain His design is itself a burning hint of His design. The riddles of God are more satisfying than the solutions of man.

God says, in effect, that if there is one fine thing about the world, as far as men are concerned, it is that it cannot be explained. He insists on the inexplicableness of everything; 'Hath the rain a father? Out of whose womb came the ice?' (46–47)

Job turned out to be Chesterton's comforting companion for most of his adult life. In 1905 he articulated very exactly how the riddles and enigmas of the universe comforted him:

Job's friends attempt to comfort him with philosophical optimism, like the intellectuals of the eighteenth century. Job tries to comfort himself with philosophical pessimism, like the intellectuals of the nineteenth century. But God comforts Job with indecipherable mystery, and for the first time Job is comforted. Eliphaz gives one answer, Job gives another answer, and the question still remains an open wound. God simply refuses to answer, and somehow, the question is answered. Job flings at God one riddle, God flings back at Job a hundred riddles, and Job is at peace. He is comforted with conundrums. For the grand and enduring idea in the poem, as suggested above, is that if we are to be reconciled to this great cosmic experience, it must be as something divinely strange and divinely violent, a quest or a conspiracy or some sacred joke. The last chapters of the colossal monologue are devoted, in a style superficially queer enough, to the detailed description of two monsters. Behemoth and Leviathan may or may not be the hippopotamus and the crocodile. But whatever they are, they are evidently embodiments of the enormous absurdity of nature. They typify that cosmic trait which anyone may see in the Zoological Gardens, the folly of the Lord which is wisdom. And in connection with one of them, God is made to utter a splendid satire upon the prim and orderly piety of the vulgar optimist. 'Wilt thou play with him as with a bird? Wilt thou bind him for thy maidens?' That is the main message of the Book of Job. Whatever this cosmic monster may be, a good animal or a bad animal, he is at least a wild animal and not a tame animal. It is a wild world and not a tame world.[10]

And Chesterton's sense of wonder too seems to have had its resonant echoes in this book of the Old Testament. He discovered, in

10 *The Speaker*, "Leviathan and the Hook" (September 7, 1905), quoted by Wills, xxv–xxvi.

Job, that God himself is astonished at what He has made:

> He unrolls before Job a long panorama of created things, the
> horse, the eagle, the raven, the wild ass, the peacock, the
> ostrich, the crocodile. The whole is a sort of psalm or rhap-
> sody of the sense of wonder. The maker of all things is
> astonished at the things He has Himself made. (48)

I would like to believe that Chesterton's mystical grace came to
him while reading the Word of God. For it is the Word of God
that cuts finely, dividing between bone and marrow, spirit and
soul (Hebrews 4:12). It was through God's paradoxical answers to
Job that Chesterton himself was comforted: "It is the lesson of
the whole work that man is most comforted by paradoxes; and it
is by all human testimony the most reassuring" (51).

It strikes me that the following remarks by Chesterton on Job
serve as an apt description of his own spiritual condition, portraying one of the main "cracks" in his spirit through which God's
merciful, mystical grace illumined his heart:

> Without once relaxing the rigid impenetrability of Jehovah
> in His deliberate declaration, he has contrived to let fall here
> and there in the metaphors, in the parenthetical imagery,
> sudden and splendid suggestions that the secret of God is a
> bright and not a sad one—semi-accidental suggestions, like
> light seen for an instant through the cracks of a closed door.
> It would be difficult to praise too highly, in a purely poetical
> sense, the instinctive exactitude and ease with which these
> more optimistic insinuations are let fall in other connec-
> tions, as if the Almighty Himself were scarcely aware that
> He was letting them out. For instance, there is that famous
> passage where Jehovah, with devastating sarcasm, asks Job
> where he was when the foundations of the world were laid,
> and then (as if merely fixing a date) mentions the time when
> the sons of God shouted for joy. One cannot help feeling,
> even upon this meager information, that they must have had
> something to shout about. Nothing could be better, artisti-
> cally speaking, than this optimism breaking through agnos-

ticism like fiery gold round the edges of a black cloud. (48–49)

The conviction that the Spirit of Religion was sweet and not bitter, and that the blaze at the back of our minds—at the back of everything—was joy and not sadness, a daydream and not a nightmare, possibly came through Chesterton's identification with Job and his meeting with Job's God. Doubting everything until he finally doubted himself, God graced him with the gift of catching the clues he dropped about the joy of the act of creation. Chesterton loved this text (Job 38:7) and referred to it frequently. But this gift which God gave him amounted to much more than just a philosophical acceptance.

The Only Serious Note in the Book: Beyond the God of the Whirlwind

I put a question mark after the title of this chapter because I believe Sunday (in *The Man Who was Thursday*) goes beyond the God of Job. Sunday certainly exemplifies many of the characteristics of Job's riddling God: "A cross between Job's riddling God in the whirlwind and the *Deus Absconditus*."[11] But Chesterton's mysticism is Christocentric, and both Job and Sunday led him to Christ. Job is ultimately a type of Christ:

> The Book of Job is chiefly remarkable, as I have insisted throughout, for the fact that it does not end in a way that is conventionally satisfactory. Job is not told that his misfortunes were due to his sins or a part of any plan for his improvement. But in the prologue we see Job tormented not because he was the worst of men, but because he was the best. It is the lesson of the whole work that man is most comforted by paradoxes. Here is the very darkest and strangest of the paradoxes; and it is by all human testimony the most reassuring. I need not suggest what a high and strange history awaited this paradox of the best man in the worst for-

---

11 Denis Conlon (ed.), "Introduction," *The Collected Works of G.K. Chesterton*, VI (San Francisco: Ignatius Press, 1991), 44.

tune. I need not say that in the freest and most philosophical sense there is one Old Testament figure who is truly a type; or say what is pre-figured in the wounds of Job.[12]

Chesterton, of course, is referring to Job's wounds as a prefigurement of Christ's wounds. The crucifixion of Christ is the most comforting reality for us because here we have the ultimate paradox—God suffering. We, of course, are one with the good thief who suffer justly for our sins. And no doubt, at the higher reaches of sanctity, one can accept all sufferings as just for even one sin against the Father. But few of us are at those heights. There is much of our suffering that is incomprehensible. What are we to do with it?

Christ on the cross is not an *explanation* of suffering, but by being united with him we can endure it with some kind of meaning which is still in the shadows of our souls. Christ is *with us* in our sufferings, even suffers with us, and he consoles and strengthens us there.

"Have You Ever Suffered?"

One of the perennial challenges hurled at God throughout the ages, and in our own time as well, is that God is sitting in his Olympian glory quite unconcerned about us. What does he know about our sufferings? What does he care?

I find the last few pages of *Thursday* the most profound of the whole book as they deal with this problem of theodicy. (Is it the ultimate meaning of the novel?) When Chesterton was asked whom he meant by Sunday he said:

I think you can take him to stand for Nature as distinguished from God. Huge, boisterous, full of vitality, dancing with a hundred legs, bright with the glare of the sun, and at first sight, somewhat regardless of us and our desires.[13]

Is Sunday the God of the "Spirit of Religion" quoted above?

---

12 Quoted by Denis Conlon, ibid., 45.
13 Ibid., 45.

It is this apparent unconcern about our human sufferings that drives many people to atheism, or worse. When Sunday is finally asked by the Secretary "Who and what are you?" He says: "I am the Sabbath. I am the peace of God." It is precisely this seeming impersonal immobility of God (who spoke "without moving") that enrages the Secretary, the type of all who shake their fist at an uncaring God:

'I know what you mean,' he cried, 'and it is exactly that that I cannot forgive you. I know you are contentment, optimism, what do they call the thing, an ultimate reconciliation. Well, I am not reconciled. If you were from the first our father and our friend, why were you also our greatest enemy? We wept, we fled in terror; the iron entered into our souls—and you are the peace of God! Oh, I can forgive God His anger, though it destroyed nations; but I cannot forgive Him His peace.'[14]

This is basically the same charge which Gregory, the real anarchist and destroyer, hurls at the conspirators sitting on their almighty thrones:

The unpardonable sin of the supreme power [the Government] is that it is supreme. I do not curse you for being cruel. I do not curse you (though I might) for being kind. I curse you for being safe! You sit in your chairs of stone, and have never come down from them. You are the seven angels of heaven, and you have had no troubles. Oh, I could forgive you everything, you that rule mankind, if I could feel for once that you had suffered for one hour a real agony such as I.

Syme cuts him off and tries to articulate how they *have suffered*. But then, wondering himself about the Secretary's own complaint against Sunday:

14 G.K. Chesterton, *The Man Who Was Thursday* (Bristol: J.W. Arrowsmith, Ltd, 1908), 322–323.

He had turned his eyes so as to see suddenly the great face of Sunday, which wore a strange smile. 'Have you,' he cried in a dreadful voice, 'have you ever suffered?' As he gazed, the great face grew to an awful size, grew larger than the awful mask of Memnon, which had made him scream as a child. It grew larger and larger, filling the whole sky; then everything went black. Only in the blackness before it entirely destroyed his brain he seemed to hear a distant voice saying a commonplace text that he had heard somewhere, 'Can ye drink of the cup that I drink of?'[15]

The voice coming out of the blackness is not unlike the voice in Job coming out of the whirlwind. The blackness—the terrible doubts: Does God care? Does God understand? Does God suffer at all? Does he know what I'm going through? Are we simply puppets of a mad Puppeteer? It is out of this blackness about to destroy his brain he hears the words of *Christ*.

In the above quote, where Chesterton is explaining who Sunday is, he concludes:

There is a phrase used at the end, spoken by Sunday: 'Can ye drink of the cup that I drink of,' which seems to mean that Sunday is God. That is the only serious note in the book, the face of Sunday changes, you tear off the mask of Nature and you find God.[16]

As part of his own dark night of the soul, when the blackness almost destroyed his own brain, surely Chesterton wrestled with this agonizing question of whether God cares or not. Job's God hurls a whole list of questions back at Job, but even this God *still doesn't seem to care all that much.* The question is only answered by the God who became one of us and now knows about suffering from his own experience. "He suffered, died, and was buried."

The God behind "the mask of Nature" is not simply the God of the Old Testament. He no longer remains aloof, hurling down stage directions from above. The key line from Chesterton's play,

---

15 Ibid., 322–329, *passim.*
16 Conlon, 45.

The Surprise, is relevant here. When the script of the perfect play God had written for Eden wasn't working out, "The Author (his head bursting out through an upper part of the scenery) says, 'And in the devil's name, what do you think you are doing with my play? Drop it! Stop! I am coming down.'"[17]

Chesterton's ultimate consoling God is not that of Job but the Just One who drank the cup to its dregs and could still say, "Father, into your hands, I commend my spirit." It is legitimate to conclude that for anyone reading this quote from the Gospel, Chesterton is saying that the ultimate explanation of this question of God's indifference to us in his peaceful Sabbath rest *can only be found in Christ*. Christ is the final revelation of the God behind the mask of nature. God suffering is the ultimate paradox.

When Job was asking God, in his admittedly tragic and religious frame of mind, "Why am I, who am a good man, suffering all this?" the riddling God did not answer with a straightforward, tract-like response such as you might find in the theology books: "You are suffering because of original sin. This means that many people, and even the forces of nature, are not in complete submission to my will as they would have been in the Garden of Eden. Trust that I love you in spite of these terrible things that are happening." And so on.

No, he did not give such a precise theological treatise. He answered, as we know, with many more questions. And in the section on the Leviathan (which my scriptural commentary says represents the chaos of the sea and any of its denizens), God's response is not prosaic but quite poetical:

> Leviathan, too! Can you catch him with a fish hook or hold his tongue down with a rope? Can you put a cane through his nostrils or pierce his jaw with a hook? Will he plead lengthily with you, addressing you in diffident tones? Will he strike a bargain with you to become your slave? Will you make a pet of him, like a bird, keep him on a lead to amuse your little girls? (Job 40:25–39)

---

17 G.K. Chesterton, *The Surprise* (New York: Sheed & Ward, 1952), 63.

As far as scripture is concerned, this is an astounding re-visioning
of reality: sitting down with the primeval monster of chaos and
discussing with him whether or not he might leave off his terrible
and uncontrollable thrashings about in the deep and become a
pet for one's daughters! God thought of it, using this kind of
speech to awaken, in a way no other expression could do, the
deeper sense of wonder in Chesterton:

> And here we may fancy that nonsense will, in a very unex-
> pected way, come to the aid of the spiritual view of things.
> Religion has for centuries been trying to make men exalt in
> the 'wonders' of Creation; but it has forgotten that a thing
> cannot be completely wonderful so long as it remains sensi-
> ble. So long as we regard a tree as an obvious thing, natu-
> rally and reasonably created for a giraffe to eat, we cannot
> properly wonder at it. It is when we consider it as a prodi-
> gious wave of the living soil sprawling up to the skies for no
> reason in particular that we take off our hats, to the aston-
> ishment of the park-keeper. Everything has in fact another
> side to it, like the moon, the patroness of nonsense. Viewed
> from that other side, a bird is a blossom broken loose from
> its chain of stalk, a man a quadruped begging on its hind
> legs, a house a gigantesque hat to cover a man from the sun,
> a chair an apparatus of four wooden legs for a cripple with
> only two.
>
> This is the side of things which tends most truly to spiri-
> tual wonder. It is significant that in the greatest religious
> poem existent, the Book of Job, the argument which con-
> vinces the infidel is not (as has been represented by the
> merely rational religionism of the eighteenth century) a pic-
> ture of the ordered beneficence of the Creation; but, on the
> contrary, a picture of the huge and undecipherable unreason
> of it. (69–70)

This is the mystic view of reality we have seen which Chesterton
expounds in *Orthodoxy,* having learned it partially from the God
of Job. One of the reasons why Chesterton's mind has influenced
millions of people is that through the inspiration and mystical
grace he received from the Book of Job and other channels, he

was able to help us, through paradox and his other forms of "nonsense," to truly *see* reality. We are surprised, delighted, amused, awed, attracted—converted even—by his presentations, because he speaks to us as God spoke to Job out of that chaotic but life-giving whirlwind:

> 'Hast Thou sent the rain upon the desert where no man is?'
> This simple sense of wonder at the shapes of things, and at their exuberant independence of our intellectual standards and our trivial definitions, is the basis of spirituality as it is the basis of nonsense. Nonsense and faith (strange as the conjunction may seem) are the two supreme symbolic assertions of the truth that to draw out the soul of things with a syllogism is as impossible as to draw out Leviathan with a hook. The well-meaning person who, by merely studying the logical side of things, has decided that 'faith is nonsense,' does not know how truly he speaks; later it may come back to him in the form that nonsense is faith. (70)

He said that "the *Iliad* is only great because all life is a battle, the *Odyssey* because all life is a journey, the *Book of Job* because all life is a riddle" (68).

The Human Club

In the mid-1890s Chesterton outlined six chapters—and wrote some of the text—of a story called "The Human Club."[18]

At the request of his heart-throb Marion, the main character, Eric Peterson, tells her the nature of his profession as a policeman: "The story is a very brief one. It has long been my belief that the greatest theoretic mistakes have arisen from the idea that the six days of Creation were over. The world is only half-quarried."[19] What human life is all about is "the gradual victory of Creation over the void."

Later, Eric meets his friend Denis Marvell, who says:

---

18 *The Collected Works of G.K. Chesterton*, XIV (San Francisco: Ignatius Press, 1993), 670–692.

19 Ibid., 674–75.

'Peterson! What good luck to meet like this. This is good luck.' 'Do not blaspheme causation,' said Peterson. 'Say rather that when the morning stars sang together and the sons of God shouted for joy, a part of their exultation was this, that this meeting of us two at this crossing was made sure.'[20]

Already in these early years (as we have seen in Chapter 2), Chesterton was mystically aware of God "immortally active" at every moment, continuing to create each day, indeed, each creature. And he was already using one of his favorite lines from Job to indicate the "blaze or burst of astonishment" behind every moment of life. (At the beginning of creation there was a burst of astonishment by the sons of God.) It is very possible that this mystical grace, embodying the awareness of on-going creation proceeding from joy and song, was the fruit of the deep personal crisis he went through at that time.

In Chesterton's writings I have frequently come across the last line of the following quote from Job, which must have held special significance for him, highlighting, as it does, the hand of God taming and limiting the chaos:

Who pent up the sea behind closed doors when it leaps tumultuous from the womb, when I wrapped it in a robe of mist and made black clouds its swaddling bands; when I cut out the place I had decreed for it and imposed gates and a bolt? 'Come so far,' I said, 'and no further; here your proud waves must break!' (38:8–11)

The Picture of Tuesday

In a very early (1896) short story entitled "The Picture of Tuesday," a group of artists are asked to draw the day of the week, Tuesday. The picture of Noel Starwood, the symbolist, is the largest:

20 Ibid., 277.

The whole was a huge human figure. Grey and gigantic, it rose with its back to the spectator. As far as the vast outline could be traced, he had one hand heaved above his head, driving up a load of waters, while below, his feet moved upon a solemn, infinite sea. It was a dark picture, but when grasped, it blinded like a sun. Above it was written 'Tuesday,' and below, 'And God divided the waters that were under the firmament from the waters that were above the firmament: and the evening and morning were the second day.'[21]

Starwood excitedly explains his artistic creation: "The week is the colossal epic of creation. Why are there not rituals for every day? The Day of the creation of Light, the Day of the Waters, the Day of the Earth, the Day of the Birds, the Day of the Beasts?"

Another artist, Middleton, thinks this is all a lot of religious nonsense. He asks Staunton, the realist, if he can think of a text for a simple, ordinary "at home day." To show that he was also thinking of his friend Job, Chesterton gives his irreligious inquirer something from Job's more pessimistic side, something more suitable to Middleton's present state of soul: "And Job lifted up his voice and cursed his day."[22]

Chesterton Not an Expert

It is a very common opinion of the "experts" that Chesterton was a poet, but not really that great; a novelist, but not really that great; a biographer, but telling more about himself than the person he was writing about; possibly a great writer of detective stories, but, and so on.

I think most would agree that he could have become great in these areas of literary endeavor, but he did not want to. Why? Because he was mystically inspired by the God of Job to see this *other side of things*, which is really the source of wonder and religion and of all the other vital elements of the human spirit. He

21 Ibid.
22 Ibid.

said of his art: "I have to carve the gargoyles because I can carve nothing else; I leave to others the angels and the arches and spires."[23]

A gargoyle, my dictionary says, "was a waterspout, often carved grotesquely, projecting at the upper part of a building, usually from the roof gutter." Chesterton carved more than gargoyles: He carved angels and saints and spires, but in the way God would have presented them to Job. He carved St. Francis tumbling around, and St. Thomas banging his fist on a table.

In his early short story, *Le Jongleur de Dieu* (mid-1890s), the laughing prophet was stoned to death lest—among other reasons—"the sweet twilight of ignorance in which all creeds live be shattered by this sudden and searching light." One of the prophet's followers had been found dead "in a great valley, amid heaps of rudely carved stones representing laughing saints, laughing prophets, laughing cherubim and seraphim, of which the maniac had been striving with his own hands to build a cathedral."[24] These are the kinds of gargoyles Chesterton would have sculptured had he a mind to do so.

I quoted Chesterton above saying that he didn't want to "keep aloof and write things that will remain in the world hundreds of years after my death." He wasn't interested in writing the perfect poem, the perfect novel, the perfect anything. He preferred, as a journalist, to turn his eye to the actual situations of daily life rather than seek the immortality of fame that might come from being a towering literary figure who wrote immortal works about cosmic issues. But, actually, he has become immortal, because he humbly remained faithful to the mystical grace he received, "by living and dying in the present stress of life as it is." By being faithful to the truth that *he saw*, and by not trying to conform to arbitrary standards of art or excellence of "the world," his works certainly will endure until the Lord comes again.

He sacrificed—probably without any regrets—the craft of the

---

23 *Alarms and Discursions*, 18. Quoted by Karen Youngberg in "Job and the Gargoyles: A Study of the Man Who Was Thursday," *The Chesterton Review*, II, 2, 1976.

24 "Public Opinion," 29 September, 1905, in Conlon, *Critical Judgments*, 18.

"expert artists" and articulated for us the life-giving truths about reality which make our souls sing and dance and laugh as did those sons of God on the first morning of creation. By remaining faithful to his grace, he gave us one of the great key to understanding reality: how to live in the present moment, in wonder and thanksgiving, and how to see God there always "immortally active," bringing everything forth instantaneously out of his unlimited power and beauty. And in this way he has indeed become immortal, winning through to his eternal goal of rest in the bosom of the riddling God, and remaining a sure guide to those of us who follow in his wake. Surely no writer has done so with more consummate genius.

12

A Different Kind of Mystic, A Different Kind of Saint

A Different Kind of Mystic

Towards the end of writing this book I re-read Maisie Ward's *Return to Chesterton* (1952).[1] She is still considered to be Chesterton's best biographer. In the introduction she states, in different words, the main thesis of this book. Neither the references to the people she quotes, nor their identity, are necessary for my purposes here. I will simply let her speak for herself. The reader will see the parallels to what I have been arguing for. Needless to say, her views about Chesterton's mysticism delighted me.

"A priest who had known Chesterton fairly well was surprised at the statement [by Chesterton in her first book *Gilbert Keith Chesterton*] that he was not an enthusiast for St. Therese of Lisieux. 'Their common vocation [he wrote to Ward], was to protest in every way they could against the mad self-sufficiency of our time. Anyhow if he did not realize that he had the same vocation as her while on earth, he is now rejoicing with her in it in heaven.'

"That these two are rejoicing together in heaven, I can well believe, but surely in comparing two very different vocations. One of the most important things about Chesterton seems to me that he came at a moment when he was tremendously needed to restore an imperiled proportion in the Christian world, to emphasize for us an element in mysticism that is sometimes forgotten.

---

1 *Return to Chesterton* (New York: Sheed and Ward, 1952). The quotes are all from her introduction (vii–xxi) unless otherwise noted.

"The especial danger today lies, I think, in the fact that one side of the Christian picture of life has been over-emphasized as part of a violent reaction against the bourgeois smugness of the last century. 'Kafka's mysticism of dejection,' wrote a reviewer, 'better suits the temper of the times than Chesterton's mysticism of happiness. It is one reason why the times are so desperately bad-tempered.'

"Looking at men who chose the mountains and not the plains of life makes the gaze dizzy, fills the mind with turbulent thoughts. St. Anthony fighting Satan in the wilderness, St. Francis singing his way in nakedness and hunger and poverty, St. Catherine speaking to such purpose after three years' silence, the pilgrim on the frozen steppes of Russia with a bag of rusks for sole sustenance repeating the cry, 'Lord Jesus Christ have mercy on me' with every breath he drew, the Cure d'Ars spending a long life in a quiet village where the devil found and fought him as he had fought Anthony in the wilderness: all these and thousands more flash into the imagination, which then turns its glance upon the daily life of millions of 'normal' people and asks: 'How can we and the saints ever live in the same heaven?'

"'We are living,' comes the answer [from Chesterton], 'on the same earth. We are living in the same world as the saints. Only they get more out of it.'

"One of the things they get out of it seems to be an unquenchable and vital gaiety. 'Saints are not sad.' It is the men who fail to reach sanctity who pours out upon us vials of their gloom. Are we really to prefer, as another reviewer would have us, 'the agonies of a Leon Bloy' to the cheerfulness of a Chesterton?

"Here we have, of course, left the high altitude of sanctity. Neither Chesterton with his ready acceptance of life's normal pleasures nor Leon Bloy with his bitter uncharity ranks with the saints—yet both men are in their fashion spiritual geniuses. The question I should like at least to open is whether Chesterton had not both the deeper and greater mysticism, mysticism closer to that of the saints, and a message far more valuable for the millions whose place is on the plains of daily effort and not on the mountains of asceticism and total renunciation.

"One would fancy from some spiritual books that there were

only two ways of dealing with life's pleasures: to refuse them or to abuse them. But in fact the task for most of us is to learn how to use them. Could we not occasionally translate the well-known phrase *terrena despicere* by the words of the Holy Ghost, 'God so loved the world'? If people try for a degree of asceticism beyond God's will for them, they usually end in a fog of unreality. And in the Rosary, which shows us the life of man as lived by God, there are ten mysteries that are joyful or glorious, but only five that are sorrowful.

"Chesterton's mysticism is a larger thing than the mysticism of suffering. It does not take the cross out of Christianity, but it sees the cross as the Tree of Life. Bloy is an introvert, a 'pilgrim of the Absolute' certainly, but a pilgrim whose own bleeding feet loom large in his consciousness. Chesterton is an extrovert, unconscious of himself to a most unusual degree.

"In England and America, while the intelligentsia may seek out the man of gloom or near-despair, the broken and unhappy seek out Chesterton. Bernard Shaw discerned the 'noble passion' for the exploited and the poor which breathed through all his [Chesterton's] writing and life. 'Even if,' writes Charles Brady, 'his ringing laughter and generous rationalism seem temporarily out of fashion, he is the one literary man of our century who has been, and still is, loved this side of idolatry.'

"Desmond MacCarthy in the *Sunday Times* noted how fully Chesterton's gratitude for existence was offered for the life that is, here and now. It is not only in the final Revelation that he sees God, but in creation: in a blade of grass, the sun in the heavens, the trees and the flowers, man and woman and the first and greatest gift of birth.

"'I am the first,' says a strange figure in a very youthful story (*A Crazy Tale*), 'that ever saw the world. Prophets and sages there have been, out of whose great hearts came schools and churches. But I am the first that ever saw a dandelion as it is.'

"'Wind and dark rain swept round, swathing in a cloud the place of that awful proclamation. I tell you religion is in its infancy, dervish and anchorite, Crusader and Ironside, were not fanatical enough or frantic enough, in their adoration. Someday a creature will be produced, a new animal with eyes to see and

THE TUMBLER OF GOD

ears to hear, with an intellect capable of performing a new function never before conceived truly; thanking God for his creation.'

"Now let us turn from the boy whose head was whirling with the sheer excitement of existence to the man writing of the great St. Thomas:

> There is a general tone and temper of Aquinas which is as difficult to avoid as daylight in a great house of windows. It is that positive position of his mind, which is filled and soaked as with sunshine with the warmth of the wonder of created things. There is a certain audacity in his communion, by which men add to their private names the tremendous titles of the Trinity and the Redemption; so that some nun may be called 'of the Holy Ghost'; or a man bear such a burden as the title of St. John of the Cross. In this sense, the man we are studying may specially be called St. Thomas of the Creation. And perhaps no man ever came so near to calling the Creation by His own name, which can only be written 'I am.'"

I simply note that Ward speaks of Chesterton's *mysticism*, and that it is *"for the millions whose place is on the plains of daily effort."* He has been given the grace of a lay mysticism for the whole Church:

> As is well known, Chesterton was not really a very church-going man, although he performed his prescribed Catholic duties. [Someone remarked that the only time he saw Chesterton angry was when he had to go to Mass very early in the morning. He said something like, "What an ungodly hour for worship."] Certainly he was not over-involved in his parish. He became holy by deeply living his vocation as a journalist. He is especially a model for laymen today.

Ward also says, referring to the many verdicts she received from her readers: "One is struck by two facts: a universal agreement that Chesterton is a very great man; the widest disagreement as to wherein that greatness lay."

My own opinion, at the end of this brief study, is that his greatness lies in the profound depth of his mind that was anointed by a mystical grace. At the end of this study, I had to ask myself: "But why was it so important to try and prove that he was a mystic, and received a mystical grace?" Mystical graces are given for others. If it can be accepted that he received a genuine mystical grace, it will add to the appreciation of what he saw with this increased vision. Those who have received mystical graces in our theological tradition used their vision to expand the mysteries of the faith and of the interior life. A mystical grace was given to Chesterton *to illuminate the daily life of people in every aspect of life.* This is a truly rare grace. I know of no other person in our whole two-thousand year tradition who had such a grace.

I believe that most of his insights in his articles in the *Illustrated London News*, for example, will be valid until the Lord comes again. Has the world ever seen such an abundance of Christian perspective on innumerable issues that span the whole of our human existence? I don't think so. He was given a mystical grace to illumine our daily lives. In this sense he was a lay mystic, and we can learn from him how to *see* in our own times.

A Different Kind of Saint

In his small book, *On the Place of Gilbert Chesterton in English Letters*, Belloc ends with these words: "We (such as I who write this) who were his companions, knew him through his very self and not through his external activity, we are in communion with him. So be it. He is in heaven."[2] In a flight of eulogistic fancy, Belloc took upon himself the charism usually reserved to the Holy Father in declaring someone to be in heaven. It is significant, nonetheless, that his last word about his friend is an affirmation about his holiness.

Chesterton says somewhere that "we need a new kind of saint." I believe that's what he was, a new kind of saint, "the first that ever saw a dandelion as it is."

There are British converts who tried to dazzle their readers with wit, erudition, and ostentatious orthodoxy, among

2 Hilaire Belloc (London: Sheed & Ward, 1940), 103.

them Robert Hugh Benson, Ronald Knox, and G.K. Chesterton. The experience of their earlier lives made these converts' view of the outside world different from that of born Catholics and enabled them to make distinctions which sometimes escaped their co-religionists.[3]

This often applies to Chesterton's ideas about the nature of holiness and sanctity, as well as other aspects of human existence. He had some different perspectives on holiness that you don't find in the traditional material. His gift of knowledge has also benefited the Church concerning this "re-visioning of holiness," especially in the area of lay holiness.

Throughout his works he gives us new and penetrating insights into the nature of holiness. These insights came from his personal striving for holiness, and from his mystical gift of knowledge that I have tried to demonstrate. As a layman immersed in the world possessing the gift of knowledge, he has given us some new wisdom about sanctity also.

I am going to take a few of his ideas about holiness and apply them to his own life. This is a kind of a vicious circle—using his own ideas about sanctity to illustrate his sanctity. I contend that mysticism gave him an awareness and understanding of holiness which only a truly holy person can possess.

Only the Church can ultimately decide both about the holiness of his life and his mystical gift. The title "Defender of the Faith" given to him by Pope Pius XI on the occasion of his death, gives a great deal of weight to the orthodoxy of his ideas in the realm of faith. The holiness he speaks about was an ideal he himself was trying to achieve, and I believe that he actually did achieve this to an extraordinary and heroic degree.

To sum up everything I want to say about the kind of holiness Chesterton taught and possessed, I could do no better than to quote a passage from *The Dumb Ox*. He was talking about the aberrations in philosophy and theology which St. Thomas and St. Francis were combating—Thomas most consciously, Francis

3 Patrick Allitt, "A New Era of Converts: From Newman and Dawson Until Today," *Crisis* (January, 1994).

less so. These errors have to do with seeking wholeness and perfection in suprahuman (Neo-platonic) or at subhuman (Manichean) levels. And then he has this marvelous statement:

> Perhaps it may be misunderstood if I say that St. Francis, for all his love of animals, saved us from being Buddhists; and that St. Thomas, for all his love of Greek philosophy, saved us from being Platonists. But it is best to say the truth in its simplest form; that they both reaffirmed the Incarnation, by bringing God back to earth.[4]

Chesterton taught and lived a more human kind of sanctity, a sanctity that can free lay people from a spirituality more suited to monks or contemplative nuns. Not that all notions of sanctity before him have suffered from inhuman doctrines (though some of them have); nor that all sanctity must be like his. But he incarnated and taught a type of sanctity which is humanly genuine and perhaps more livable by the laity. He has lived and taught some new expressions of holiness. He wedded human nature to Christian love and truth in new heroic ways. He brought mysticism back to earth.

All the objections to his sanctity will be found in a lack of understanding that his kind of holiness was deeply incarnational—white hot for the truth about the world we live in, and on fire with love for humanity. His love for the things of the world—food, for example—did not make him lose his love for the God who created all these things and found them good.

Another short quote which also represents and sums up his kind of holiness is found in *St. Francis*: "St. Francis was a lover of man, a possibly rarer mystical vocation." Chesterton really loved people to an extraordinary degree. He deeply loved all the Shaws and Wells of the world, even though he disagreed with them. He loved the Pope and the postman. And one morning when the cat was eating out of his plate, he would not allow the maid to shoo the cat away. He said he didn't mind sharing breakfast with her. He loved the world in the sense scripture says that "God so loved the world."

---

4 *St. Thomas Aquinas*, 29.

Some of the things I know about his life, and many of his notions about holiness, I find more challenging than many sayings of the desert fathers, or writings of the saints. For example, he said, "Every person is interesting." Do I really believe every person is interesting and worth knowing? Did St. Anthony of the Desert believe that? Human relations—the mysticism of loving people—is probably the hardest challenge of all.

I believe Chesterton most identified with St. Thomas among all the saints. Consequently, I find his thoughts on sanctity from *St. Thomas, The Dumb Ox* most congenial to understanding his own holiness. We find in that book an elaboration of his own sense of mission, his own ideal of holiness:

> Every saint is a man before he is a saint; and a saint may be made of every sort or kind of man; and most of us will choose between these different types according to our different tastes. But I will confess that, while the romantic glory of St. Francis has lost nothing of its glamour for me, I have in later years grown to feel almost as much affection, or in some respects even more, for the man who unconsciously inhabited a large heart and a large head, like one inheriting a large house, and exercised there an equally generous if rather more absent-minded hospitality. There are moments when St. Francis, the most unworldly man who ever walked the world, is almost too efficient for me.[5]
>
> Yes, in spite of the contrasts that are as conspicuous and even comic as the comparison between the fat man and the thin man, these two great men [Francis and Thomas] were doing the same great work; one in the study and the other in the street. They were not bringing something new into Christianity, in the sense of something heathen or heretical into Christianity; on the contrary, they were bringing Christianity into Christendom.[6]

I believe Chesterton's achievement in the world of the mind is equal to that of a Doctor of the Church. He was bringing Chris-

5 Ibid., 22–23.
6 Ibid.

tianity back into Christendom (to use a euphemism about the society of his day) and that this is how he saw his mission and talents. We might say that he was doing the work of the mind in the street. Any evaluation of his sanctity must be centered here. Every saint is unique. What attracts us about them is that they are inimitable: we can never be exactly like them, but their uniqueness is an inspiration for us.

The Lord gives us the saints we need, not necessarily those we want or even understand.

> A saint is a medicine because he is an antidote. Indeed that is why the saint is often a martyr; he is mistaken for a poison because he is an antidote. He will generally be found restoring the world to sanity by exaggerating whatever the world neglects, which is by no means always the same element in every age. Yet each generation seeks its saint by instinct; and he is not what the people want, but rather what the people need. Therefore it is the paradox of history that each generation is converted by the saint who contradicts it most.[7]

How is the saintly Chesterton an antidote to the modern world? What need does he fill? He is one of the thinkers who most contradicts the present generation. In an age when too many people consider material things are the only reality, Chesterton, with his mystical gift of knowledge, showed how the material creation must be seen with the transcendent eye. And he did this, not by writing deep tracts from a monastic cell detached from the world, but precisely by being immersed in the world and talking about all the things of the world with a faith vision. He wanted to remain passionately in the world, reflecting on the everyday events in which ordinary people must live. In short, "he loved the world."

An English Urodivoi

There is a type of saint among the Russians called urodivoi, "holy fools." We have them in the West as well—Benedict Joseph Labre, for instance. They consciously acted foolish to atone for

---

7 Ibid., 23–24.

the ridicule and humiliation suffered by Christ. They often became beggars, or allowed themselves to be seen and known as madmen or madwomen. St. Basil's Cathedral in Moscow is actually named after St. Basil the Fool, and not the great Bishop of Cappadocia.

Chesterton says somewhere that "the thin monks were holy but the fat monks were humble, because to be laughed at is much better for the human condition." This is an interesting distinction he makes between holiness and humility. I'm sure he also thought the thin monks were humble—but not as humble as they could be. His joy and frivolity were part of his humility. He would have found the seriousness of many of the saints not humble enough. In relationship to the Creator, how can you take yourself too seriously! He is the Innocent Smith of *Manalive* who does preposterous things to see the world from a different perspective and, what is more, to get others to re-vision the often dull reality into which they have locked themselves.

Chesterton experienced something of the perfect joy of St. Francis by being laughed at for his weight, and by poking fun at his own foibles. He did and said outlandish things—not to camouflage his sanctity: that kind of duplicity would have been foreign to his simplicity and honesty. He would simply have thought that these preposterous ways of acting are normal for those who are filled with the exuberance of the divine life, for those who realize something of what it means to be constantly coming forth from the Creator's hand. Gide, who had met him once, said, "He was such a happy man that you would think he had found God."

The Song of Solomon

From Chesterton's vast writings it would be easy to prove that his influence on the Catholic world was immense. "But"—the objection comes—"that doesn't mean he had a great loving heart as well as a great mind. Isn't holiness a matter of love? His life was all in his head! Where are the great outpourings of his love for God as we find in the writings of the saints?"

I have treated, in the chapter on St. Thomas, the theological certainty that God is truth as well as love. In the Office for Doctors, the Church recognizes this connection between teaching the truth and holiness of life: "Those who are learned will be as radiant as the sky in all its beauty; those who instruct the people in goodness will shine like the stars for all eternity." If a Vincent de Paul spends his life in active charity, we conclude he was holy. If a St. Francis Xavier pours out his life in missionary activity, we conclude he was filled with zeal to an heroic degree. If abundant truth pours forth from someone's lips, we say, "It's only in his head"! Why? If we say, "God is Love," and whoever loves knows God, can we not also say, "God is truth, and whoever has truth possesses God"? "The just man will speak the wisdom he has pondered in his heart."

Again, only the Church can decide this. But Chesterton gives us some clues in *The Dumb Ox* on how to go about looking at his own life; but he certainly didn't mean to provide these criteria for us for examining his own life.

I don't find in Chesterton great outpourings about his love for God such as we find in the writings of many of the saints. Chesterton says the following about St. Thomas, which I would apply to himself:

It is true that the mystics and the men of the Franciscan school dwelt more lovingly on the admitted supremacy of love. But it was mostly a matter of emphasis; perhaps tinged faintly by temperament; possibly in the case of St. Thomas, a shadowy influence of a sort of shyness. Whether the supreme ecstasy is more affectionate than intellectual is no very deadly matter of quarrel among men who believe it is both, but do not profess even to imagine the actual experience of either. But I have a sort of feeling that, even if St. Thomas had thought it was as emotional as St. Bonaventure did, he would never have been so emotional about it. It would always have embarrassed him to write about love at such length. All sanctity is secrecy; and his sacred poetry was really a secretion, like the pearl in a very tightly closed oyster.[8]

And speaking of the last moments of St. Thomas:

8 Ibid., 138–139.

It may be worth remarking, for those who think that he thought too little of the emotional or romantic side of religious truth, that he asked to have the Song of Solomon read through to him from beginning to end.[9]

There was a shyness in Chesterton about his deep personal life with God. The saints refer to "the secrets of the King," communications that are too deep for words, even for those gifted with words. Or, more to the point, too personal to share with anyone except the Lover.

Did you ever wonder why we have so very few autobiographies of the thousands of saints on the calendar? How many autobiographies could you name? Six or so? And many of these were written under obedience—The Story of a Soul by St. Therese, for example. The saints, generally, were very secretive about their lives with God. "All sanctity is secrecy." The word martyr, he reminds us, means witness. But when it comes to the saints' inner life with God, a lover's secrecy comes into play.

What Chesterton said of the joy of Christ at the end of Orthodoxy, we could say of his love affair with God: It was something too great to be shown on earth. He hid it under laughter—not "running laughter" like in the Hound of Heaven—but the laughter of one who really had found God and was genuinely happy. It was not a nervous laughter; it was the laughter of the saints.

A Child of Five

Chesterton speaks about the last confession of Aquinas: "The confessor, who had been with him in the inner chamber, ran forth as if in fear, and whispered that his confession had been that of a child of five."[10]

This last phrase always sort of chokes me up. For Thomas, despite his incredible greatness of intellect, had also achieved what Jesus said was indispensable for entrance into the kingdom, to become a little child.

9 Ibid., 142.
10 Ibid., 143.

And does not Chesterton strike us in exactly the same way? He who possessed one of the deepest minds in the history of the world, was he not a child? He loved and played with children. He said the toy theatre was the greatest of all games. He threw paper birds out to the children as he worked on his trifles of thought. His amazing sense of wonder, as if he saw things every day for the first time—is this not a characteristic of the child? He said once that if a door opens and someone comes in, the adult looks at the person whereas the child is just amazed at the door opening. And was he not, up to his death, continually amazed at each new door opening in his life, swinging it back and forth just like a child, and marveling at the newness of everything?

He was asked once why he joined the Catholic Church. "Why, to have my sins forgiven. Why else!" A man who saw forgiveness of sins as the prime reason for his entrance into the Church, and as the greatest motive of gratitude towards his Creator, perhaps also confessed at the last as a child of five.

"He Will Lose His Ecumenical Effectiveness!"

Objections to opening any kind of cause for Chesterton are many. One that has arisen in my own mind, and I'm sure in the minds of others, is that if Chesterton is canonized he will become "Catholic property" and lose his appeal to those outside the Church. I know this is a fear among Catholics, but I don't know if it is a real problem for those not of our faith. We tend these days to be super-sensitive as to how people view the Catholic faith. Often it's a projection of our own attitudes.

I'm thinking of countless thousands of people down through the ages who were converted to the faith by reading Catholic authors. If you are searching for the truth, you're going to read approved and recognized—and, yes, even canonized—authors. Do we have to apologize for our pointing to certain people and saying, "We consider these people holy, and their works are excellent guides to our faith." When Jacques Maritain was looking around for truth before committing suicide, he turned to St. Thomas Aquinas. I don't think the fact that Thomas had been canonized interfered with Maritain's reading of his writings. I think those seeking the truth would like to know which people the Church considers both good guides to her faith.

Edith Wyschogrod in her book *Saints and Postmodernism*, says that ethical theories have become so hopelessly confused and complicated that the lives of the saints can serve as a living, normative pattern for peoples' search for the meaning of life. This is how she puts it:

> A postmodern ethic must look not to some opposite of ethics but elsewhere, to life narratives, specifically those of saints, defined in terms that defy the normative structure of moral theory.[11]

The lives of saints communicate the Christian reality in a direct and unambiguous way. Saints are an alternative way of offering to the modern world patterns of goodness and morality that anyone can understand and be guided by. The life of St. Francis has probably influenced more lives than all the ethical textbooks on earth!

I hope that someday in the new millennium Chesterton will be canonized. And I hope that the artists who sculpt statues of him and draw his "holy pictures" will represent him as he was: not too fat, but heavy; not laughing, but smiling slightly; and I'd prefer him with his cape and sword cane.

In closing this little volume I can't help borrowing the story told by William Oddie at the beginning of his talk at that June, 2009 Conference in Oxford.

> Just after Chesterton's premature death at the age of 62, Maisie Ward, his first biographer, a friend of 30 years, was touched by a tribute paid to him by the maid at a house he used to visit in his home town of Beaconsfield. With tears in her eyes, she said simply, 'Oh, Miss. Our Mr. Chesterton dying—he was sorter a saint, Miss, wasn't he? Just to look at him when you handed him his hat made you feel sorter awesome.'[12]

---

11 (Chicago and London: University of Chicago Press, 1990), xiii.
12 *The Catholic Herald*, "The Holiness of Chesterton," 23 May, 2010.

What will his name be when he is canonized? "St. Gilbert of the Flaming Pen" or "St. Gilbert of the Presence" or "St. Gilbert of the Creator"? But he certainly wouldn't want any of these "tremendous titles." Chesterton believed that his greatest dignity was just to be an ordinary man. In England they have St. Julian *of Norwich*, St. John *of Bridlington*, and St. Thomas *of Canterbury*. So why not simply, "St. Gilbert of Beaconsfield"?

Gilbert, pray for us in this Third Millennium, that we may have the wisdom and knowledge to see all human reality in the divine light. Pray that we may have the courage to fight the dragons with the same zeal and love with which you fought. Pray that we may be harbingers of the second spring, never losing hope. Obtain for us fidelity in the battle, even when the task seems hopeless. Help us to place our hope in the risen Christ, in him (as you once so beautifully said) "who knows his way back from the dead."

Bibliography

Augustine, Saint. *The Confessions of St. Augustine*. Hyde Park, NY: New City Press, 1997.

Balthasar, Hans Urs von. *The Glory of the Lord*. San Francisco: Ignatius Press, 1984.

Belloc, Hilaire. *On the Place of Gilbert Chesterton in English Letters*. London: Sheed & Ward, 1940.

Benedict XIV, Pope. *Heroic Virtue: A Portion of the Treatise of Benedict XIV on the Beatification and Canonization of the Servants of God.* Trans. by the English Fathers of the Oratory. London: Thomas Richardson and Son, 1850.

Blake, William. *The Penguin Poets*. New York: Penguin, 2005.

Boyd, Ian. "Chesterton and the Bible." *The Chesterton Review* (XI, No. 1).

Catherine of Siena, Saint. *The Dialogue*. New York: Paulist Press, 1980.

Chesterton, G.K. *Alarms and Discursions*. New York: Dodd, Mead and Co., 1911.

_____. *Autobiography*. New York: Sheed & Ward, 1936.

_____. *The Catholic Church and Conversion*. New York: The Macmillan Company, 1929.

_____. *Collected Works of G.K. Chesterton*, ed. Denis Conlon. San Francisco: Ignatius, 1991.

_____. *The Coloured Lands*. New York: Sheed & Ward, 1938.

_____. *The Critical Judgments*, ed. Denis Conlon. Antwerp: University Faculty of St. Ignatius, 1976.

_____. *The Defendant*. New York: Classic Books, 2000.

_____. *The Everlasting Man*. New York: Dodd, Mead & Co, 1925.

_____. *St. Francis of Assisi*. New York: George H. Doran Co., 1924.

_____. *St. Francis of Assisi*. Mineola, NY: Dover Publications, Inc., 2008.

_____. *Heretics*. New York: Dodd, Mead & Co., 1925.

_____. *The Man Who Was Thursday*. Bristol: J.W. Arrowsmith, Ltd, 1908.

_____. *Orthodoxy*. New York: Sheed & Ward, 1936.

_____. *Orthodoxy*. Thomas More Press: Chicago, 1985.

_____. *The Resurrection of Rome*. London: Hodder and Stoughton, Ltd, 1934.

_____. *A Short History of England*. New York: John Lane Company, 1917.

Bibliography

_____. *St. Thomas Aquinas*. New York: Image, Doubleday, 1956.

_____. *St. Thomas Aquinas*. London: Hodder & Stoughton, 1933.

_____. *William Blake*. New York: Duckworth & Co., 1910.

_____. *The Works of G. K. Chesterton*. Hertfordshire: Wordsworth Editions, 1995.

Conlon, Denis, ed. *G. K. Chesterton: A Half-Century of Views*. New York: Oxford University Press, 1987.

_____. *The Chesterton Review* (Vol. II, No.1, Fall–Winter, 1975).

Fonseka, J.P. de, ed. *G. K. C. as M. C.* London: Methuen & Co. Ltd, 1929.

_____. *Select Essays and Verses of J.P. de Fonseka*, ed. Leonard Obris. Waikkal, Sri Lanka: Leonard Obris, 1989.

Garrigou-Lagrange OP, Reginald. *Three Ages of the Interior Life*. St. Louis: B. Herder Book Co., 1957.

Grist, Anthony. "A Contrast in Mysticism." *The Chesterton Review* (Vol. XVI, No. 3–4, Aug.–Nov., 1990).

Hetzler, Leo. "Chesterton's Teen-Age Writings." *The Chesterton Review* (Vol. II, No.1).

John Paul II, Pope. *Crossing the Threshold of Hope*. New York: Alfred A. Knopf, 1994.

Katz, Steven T., ed. *Mysticism and Religious Traditions*. Oxford University Press, 1983.

Kenner, Hugh. *Paradox in Chesterton*. New York: Sheed & Ward, 1947.

Knowles, David. *The Nature of Mysticism*. New York: Hawthorn Books, 1966.

Lauer SJ, Quentin. *G. K. Chesterton, Philosopher Without Portfolio*. New York: Fordham University Press, 1988.

MacDonald, George. *Lilith*. Grand Rapids: Eerdmans, 1981.

Mackey, Aidan. "Chesterton, Fidei Defensor." *30 Days* (October, 1989).

Martindale, C. C. *The Life of Robert Hugh Benson*. Bibliographical Center for Research, 2010.

McCann, Dom Justin, ed. *The Cloud of Unknowing*. London: Burns & Oates, 1943.

McGinn, Bernard. *Foundations of Mysticism*. New York: The Crossroad Publishing Company, 1994.

Nichols OP, Aidan. *Chesterton as Theologian*. London: Darton-Longman-Todd, 2009.

Nimmo, Duncan. *Reform and Division in the Franciscan Order*. Rome: Capuchin Historical Institute, 1987.

O'Donoghue, Noel. "Chesterton's Marvelous Boyhood." *The Chesterton Review* (Vol. 6, No. 1, Fall–Winter 1979–80).

Oakes, Edward T. 'Philosophy in an Old Key." *First Things* (Dec., 2000).

Oddie, William, ed. *The Holiness of G. K. Chesterton*. Herefordshire: Gracewing, 2010.

Pearce, Joseph. *Wisdom and Innocence: A Life of G. K. Chesterton*. London: Hodder & Stoughton Ltd, 1996.

Plotinus. *Enneads*, trans. Stephen MacKenna. New York: Penguin, 1991.

Pramuk, Christopher. *Sophia: the Hidden Christ of Thomas Merton*. Collegeville, MN: The Liturgical Press, 2009.

Rahner, Karl. *The Practice of Faith*. New York: Crossroad, 1992.

Schindler, David L. *Heart of the World, Center of the Church*. Grand Rapids, MI: Eerdmans, 1996.

Schweitzer, Albert. *Mysticism of Paul the Apostle*. Baltimore: Johns Hopkins University Press, 1998.

Underhill, Evelyn. *Mysticism*. New York: Image Books, Doubleday, 1990.

Varghese, Roy Abraham. *The Wonder of the World: A Journey from Modern Science to the Mind of God*. Fountain Hills, AZ: Tyr Publishing, 2003.

Ward, Maisie. *Gilbert Keith Chesterton*. New York: Sheed & Ward, 1943.

_____. *Return to Chesterton*. New York: Sheed and Ward, 1952.

Wills, Garry. *Chesterton, Man and Mask*. New York: Sheed & Ward, 1961.

Wyschogrod, Edith. *Saints and Postmodernism*. Chicago: University of Chicago Press, 1990.

Yeats, W.B. *Essays and Introductions*. London: Macmillan 1961.

Youngberg, Karen. "Job and the Gargoyles: A Study of the Man Who Was Thursday." *The Chesterton Review* (II, 2, 1976).

INDEX OF NAMES

Index of Names

CPSIA information can be obtained at www.ICGtesting.com
Printed in the USA
LVOW080406050713

341508LV00013B/794/P